Emerging Media

Emerging Media

Legal Principles, Virtual Issues

Jason Zenor

State University of New York at Oswego

Bassim Hamadeh, CEO and Publisher
Todd R. Armonstrong, Publisher
Tony Paese, Project Editor
Alia Bales, Production Editor
Abbie Goveia, Graphic Design Assistant
Trey Soot, Licensing Coordinator
Natalie Piccotti, Director of Marketing
Kassie Graves, Vice President of Editorial
Jamie Giganti, Director of Academic Publishing

3970 Sorrento Valley Blvd., Ste. 500, San Diego, CA 92121

Brief Contents

Detailed Contents

Preface

This book introduces undergraduates to the *nexus between communication law* and *emerging media technology*. Whereas most communication law books are geared toward students entering the traditional professions of journalism or broadcasting, this book is aimed at undergraduates in *contemporary media and information studies* who face a more disrupted media environment. Unlike other communication law books in the market, this book focuses exclusively on communication technologies that are central to all students who will spend their entire lives as consumers and citizens.

This book provides a *clear and simple overview of communication law*. It is not case or citation heavy nor does it delve into the mechanics of the legal system and cases. Instead this book focuses on introducing students to legal and policy issues. Thus, the chapters present legal doctrines in accessible terms and always in the context of current issues and technology. The text provides a litany of current examples and a legal analysis of how they could be resolved. Each chapter ends with a case study and discussion questions so students can apply the legal doctrine to a communication technology problem.

This book results from a decade of teaching media law courses. Over the years, my students have changed; thus, the course has changed. They no longer watch linear television. In fact, most of their media consumption is in the form of short videos from YouTube and TikTok. They are more interested in gaming and technology than they are with television and movies. They are very attuned to what is going on in the world, but they are not consuming traditional journalism on television news or reading the *New York Times* online.

As a result, a course designed around a traditional communication law textbook seems out of date. Having students learn all the intricate details about a filing a lawsuit, FCC broadcasting regulations, or ways to file a FOIA request seems out of touch with their interests and needs. Over the last decade, the best part of my media law classes have been the discussions and debates on current issues in their communication environment. The topics of these discussions have evolved from the concepts listed above to focusing on more pertinent issues like fake news, doxing, data breaches, creepy sex robots, and the power of tech companies. Thus, the goal of this book is to be the next step in the evolution of communication law textbooks by *reflecting the media environment in which today's students live.*

Finally, this book differs from others on the market because of its larger focus on *legal and policy issues* with communication technology. Some of these issues are present today, and students are well-aware of them. Other issues are looming, but foreseeable. The idea is to prompt our students to think critically about the potential psychological, social, and political harms that communication technology can cause. With an underlying foundation in legal doctrines, students can begin to consider the best approaches to solving these issues. Ultimately, this book is unique on the market because it moves beyond memorizing the intricacies and nuances of legal doctrine to having student apply *critical thinking* to pressing issues of law and technology.

Acknowledgments

I would like to thank all of those who have helped me over the course of this project. First, I would like to thank the Communication Studies Department and the School of Communication, Media, and the Arts at SUNY-Oswego for giving me the time and support to write this book. I want to give a special shout out to my colleague Jennifer Fogel for reading an initial draft and offering helpful critiques. I would also like to thank two students from our department who worked with me as research assistants: Amada Caba and Rachelle Hills. They spent countless hours scouring the internet and legal sites to make sure the book was up to date on examples of legal issues concerning technology.

I want to thank Todd Armstrong and Tony Paese of Cognella Publishing for their guidance throughout the course of this project. Their expertise and advice helped me get to the finish line. No matter how much my procrastination and scatter-brain got in the way, they were always supportive.

I would also like to thank the following manuscript reviewers: Brian L. Frye (College of Law, University of Kentucky), Mike Igoe (Department of Communication, State University of New York at Fredonia), Steven Kirkland (Jack J. Valenti School of Communication, University of Houston), Jared Schroeder (Department of Journalism, Meadows School of the Arts, Southern Methodist University), and Joseph P. Staniunas, Jr. (School of Communication, Radford University). Their comments and critiques gave me a fresh perspective on how to shape this into a more significant and fruitful project. To all those who assisted and gave opinions on the book, I am beyond grateful. It should also be made clear that the arguments made in this book reflect the opinions of the author, and any remaining errors are, of course, my responsibility alone.

Finally, I have a few personal notes of gratitude. First to my parents, who would often take my children for the day so I could do research and write. Watching four children is insane at any age. Most of all, I would like to thank my wife Rebecca for putting up with my whining over the 2 years of this project. I am available to watch Netflix now.

CHAPTER 1

Thinking About Emerging Media and Law

O ver the decades, science fiction has made many predictions about the future—some were right, while some were just wrong. One such example is the movie *Blade Runner* (1982) starring Harrison Ford in a dystopian future in the distant year of 2019. (In 2017, Harrison Ford and Ryan Gosling starred in the sequel titled *Blade Runner: 2049*.) The movie had to predict some technological advances that would occur in under 40 years. It foresaw flying cars and robot clones called replicants. Of course, those advances have yet to come to fruition. But it also predicted correctly that people would be video chatting through phones and talking to computers in their homes (Trammell, 2018). Other science fiction writers have also been prescient; for example, George Orwell wrote about thimble-sized audio players reminiscent of today's ear buds. Arthur C. Clarke created "newspads," which were like iPads, and he also described virtual reality gaming (Willett, 2018). What was once a crazy science fiction story is now our reality.

Technology is advancing fast. It seems like what we recently considered to be "new technology" is now commonplace. Virtual reality devices, talking AI in our homes, and life-like robots are no longer a novelty. This technology has certainly enriched our lives by providing infinite information, offering countless hours of entertainment, and connecting us to the broader world. The benefits from this technology are so great that attempting to list them all would be a futile effort.

At the same time, there are costs to this technology such as massive data breaches, spreading of misinformation, and biased judgments of algorithms, to name just a few. We usually become aware of these issues through the alarmist clickbait on our social media feeds. As incidents become more frequent, the issues soon enter into our political debates, until there is a call for action to stop the problems. If the problems persist, then the government steps in to offer solutions.

A recent example of this debate has been Congressional hearings on tech companies' use of data. For years, the public's concern about online privacy had been growing. Whistleblowers had exposed widespread government surveillance. There were revelations about how social media companies tracked and sold users' data. Then, in 2018, news broke that the company Cambridge Analytic had been collecting and using data from millions of Facebook accounts without the users' consent. Political campaigns had been using the information for persuasive purposes. This was the tipping point. Public outrage now became loud enough that legislators were forced to act. The government threatened policy changes and direct regulation of the industry. The tech companies responded by making some changes to data protection, although advocacy groups have argued that the changes are not enough (Ivanova, 2018).

The issue of online privacy is not new. Scholars and critics have been concerned about it for more than 30 years, dating back to the first data-tracking cookies on the internet. But with the advent of technologies such as the Apple iPhone and social media at the end of the early 2000s, privacy issues became even greater. Smartphones gave people consistent internet access throughout the day outside of their homes, so they were online more. With social media, people began putting more and more information online for public viewing. In the early days of Facebook, people rushed to join their friends in the new virtual space without giving much thought to the data they were sharing (Johnson, 2010).

It is safe to say that had we thought ahead and analyzed the emerging communication technology and its consequences, we might have been better prepared to solve problems when they did occur. Unfortunately, we often wait until the problems are too big before we start to consider solutions. We are then stuck in overreactions and laying blame, with actual policy solutions taking a back seat.

This chapter outlines the emerging communication technology and our approach to analyzing it throughout the book. First, it discusses the history of new technology causing social panics and calls for regulations. Second, it describes the three broad categories of communication technology covered throughout the book. Finally, it analyzes the shortcoming of using only legal solutions to try and solve every issue caused by technological changes.

New Technology, New Problems, New Law?

There is a noticeable trend in responses to new technology. A new techno-logical tool brings great excitement and hope. It has the power to extend and enrich lives. At the same time, the new technology introduces new and abrupt changes, which creates fear. Then the technology becomes the scapegoat for social ills (Herrman, 2017).

The evolution of **communication technology** illustrates this cycle. The printing press enabled easy duplication of books, which could then be spread across the world. This spread shifted power away from a small set of clergy and royalty and to a growing merchant class. It is no coincidence that this transfer of power coincided with the Renaissance and the evolution in the sciences, the arts, and government (Whipps, 2008). Of course, those who were in power were not as excited by the change and often fought back against the democratization of information by imprisoning and even murdering those who dissented.

In the 1800s, the telegraph and photography (and later film) become available to the public. These inventions coincided with the great changes of the Industrial Revolution and growth of international relations. But they also created concerns about privacy (Warren and Brandeis, 1890) and obscenity (e.g., Comstock Act of 1873), and prompted some irrational fears, such as the claim that photographs would steal a person's image (Crowley, 2014). The rise of photography led to privacy laws to protect people from having their image used without their consent.

Electronic communication, such as radio and television, became common in the beginning of 20th century. It allowed news and entertainment to spread across the world. But it was also seen as a powerful tool coopted by gov-ernments for propaganda purposes (Little, 2016). The rise of broadcasting networks led to a public system of licensed stations that had to follow the Federal Communications Commission rules on indecency and equal time.

Finally, post-WWII saw the development of computers and the internet, which provided access to an infinite amount of information and the ability to have social connections across the world. But, at the same, there has been continuing fear about this digital technology because it allows for information bubbles and echo chambers, which have led to tribalism, extremism, and a call for tougher regulations (Illing, 2018).

Today, the way we communicate with each other is changing rapidly because of advancing technology. These changes will surely lead to great things, but they will also cause some problems and subsequent calls for regulation. The following section outlines the types of emerging technology and some of the prevailing issues to be considered throughout this book.

Emerging Communication Technology

Terms such as *media* and *technology* are often indeterminate and can be so ambiguous that everything is included. For example, people still use ham (amateur) radios and fax machines, which are media (a channel for mass communication) and a technology. To narrow it down, in this book, we examine only **emerging communication technology**.

Emerging communication technology is defined as media-related products that became commercial in the 21st century. Most of the technology is not as well established as other media such as radio and televisions, which have almost universal market penetration. Some technology may be for sale, while others may be available only to a limited market that can afford to use them. Some technology is still in its infancy and may develop to be quite different in a few years. Nonetheless, it is technology that enhances our communication ability. It satisfies the same uses and gratifications provided by traditional media such as books, radio, and television. For the purposes of this book, emerging communication technology has been divided into three broad categories: connected devices, virtual reality, and artificial intelligence.

Connected Devices and the Internet of Things

The **Internet of Things** (**IoT**) is a term used to describe the millions of connected devices people use every day. Many common devices—from televisions to watches to home appliances—are connected to each other and can be controlled through the internet or apps. These devices record information that can be sent to other devices through a network. The information may be stored locally or shared through **cloud computing**. Information stored "in the cloud" may be saved in a public or private network of remote servers with varying security properties (Knorr, 2018).

The list of connected or smart devices is countless, but examples include cell phones, televisions, gaming consoles, digital assistants, watches, cars, refrigerators, washing machines, and security systems. Some devices are large consumer goods, but anything with a chip can be connected, even a device as small as a grain of rice. In fact, some people have had chips inserted in their bodies and are monitored through the IoT (Graham, 2017).

Connected devices record and share the information of our lives—from our habits to our movements to our activities. The information is often mundane, the type of information we would regularly share with others—like what we watch on television or like to eat. Some of the information is public, but was unrecorded a decade or two ago, such as purchases, travel routes, and our location (Nakashima, 2018). But some of the information is more private like conversations, security codes, and health information (Dargin, 2017). A connected device can regularly record this information and store it in the cloud because we often have consented to this recording and storing just by using the device.

Scholars estimate that the amount of traffic on the IoT is 15 quintillion bytes or about the equivalent of 750,000 years' worth of digital video (Marr, 2018). This information can range from the individual level to **big data** sets, which compile information from thousands to millions of users. In turn, this information can be used to improve our lives. For example, we can monitor our health through smart watches, and our health data can be shared with doctors. Planners can track the movement of traffic in a city to design better routes. Farmers can monitor crops and livestock to increase efficiency yields. But there are also concerns about the extent of our connected world and the information tech companies collect. The main issues with IoT relate to surveillance and privacy (discussed in Chapter 5), but other concerns discussed in this book include recording of sexual activity (Chapter 7) and the commoditization of data (Chapter 9).

Virtual and Augmented Reality

Reality is the totality of what our brains sense from the environment around us. Through sight, sound, smell, taste, and touch, we determine our world. But the stimulus does not have to be a physical interaction. Any information our senses record creates the world in we live in. Thus, the essence of virtual reality is to develop an artificial world with enough information that it tricks our senses into experiencing it as "reality" (May, 2017).

Virtual reality (**VR**) is a 3-dimensional environment created through computer graphics. When it is a hybrid of a natural environment and a computer-generated environment, then it is called **augmented reality** (**AR**), which this book includes as part of the VR environment. Video games have long created an alternative environment in which players operate, but it was always 2-dimensional and clearly simulated. The objective of VR is to make the simulation as near to reality as possible, although some games still rely on fantasy or arcade-like graphics as part of their value to the consumer. VR is now becoming a commercial reality. Companies such as Facebook and Samsung are selling gear for the public to use, and content is being created in entertainment, news, and sports.

VR is used to create an immersive experience for the user, giving it potentiality in many areas of life and business. Consumers are aware of the ways it can make entertainment more exciting. It can also give them a more expansive picture for learning information. For example, *The Guardian* offered a series of stories about the negative effects of solitary confinement that allowed a user to experience it through VR. By simulating the real-world, VR can enable people to train safely for dangerous jobs like space travel, law enforcement, and military. It can be used to lessen the effects of PTSD by simulating the experiences that triggered it (Lake, 2017). But, there are also concerns about the negative effects of VR (LaMotte, 2017). Critics argue that the simulated experience may be too realistic and too immersive. The main issues with VR discussed in this book arenegligence (Chapter 6), moral harms (Chapter 7), and control over identity (Chapter 8).

Artificial Intelligence

When we think of **artificial intelligence**, we usually think of robots that appear to be human. But that is not the current reality. These days, we are surrounded by artificial intelligence, mostly in the form of the algorithms used in social media, streaming, and other websites. Simply put, artificial intelligence is any machine that has been programmed to learn. The software can process large amounts of information in order to complete a task, whether it is recommending a song to a person or driving a car. But AI can now go beyond simple learning and solve complex problems akin to natural intelligence (Foy, 2018).

AI has many applications. It is used to assist doctors in diagnostics and by businesses to help uncover complex financial crimes. The U.S. military uses AI-controlled drones to fly intelligence missions (Pawlyk, 2019). But there are, once again, concerns about this technology. Because AI is designed by humans to learn from humans, it could adopt implicit biases and racial profiling. Bad actors with malicious intent could program AI to do terrible things such as hacking. Critics of AI's advancement warn of machines replacing humans and the loss of ethical decision making (Brown, 2017). Some of the main concerns with AI discussed in this book include the spreading of misinformation (Chapter 4), surveillance (Chapter 5), and liability (Chapter 6).

Values and Consequences of Emerging Media Law

In its examination of the issues that surround emerging communication technology, this book's approach is to put the concerns in the context of legal principles. The idea is that solutions to these problems will be found in our policy, laws, and courts. The hope is that, in the following chapters, you come to understand the major doctrines in communication law. You will also be alerted to the current and foreseeable issues that may arise from our adoption of new technology. Ultimately, the goal is for you to be able to critically assess these issues and deliberate on the possible solutions in the context of current law.

But, admittedly, law is not always the answer. Law is often the minimum a person must do. It is a punitive system, and many of us follow the law just to avoid punishment, not because it is the right thing to do. What we should be doing and what is in the public interest is often a matter of morals or ethics.

Ethics are the rules that we should follow, but they are not the law. Sometimes, they are explicit, like with a code of ethics for an occupation. Other times, they are social norms that we are supposed to learn through experience. Then sometimes, they are individual duties that we believe must be followed. Ethics are, in many ways, the behaviors we exercise based on our morals and values.

Law and ethics are similar. They are both a set of rules that govern behavior and conduct. They both deal with what we believe to be right or wrong. The optimal law should live up to our ethics, but often it does not. If law is the minimum standard we must follow, then ethics are the ideal for which we should strive.

The study of ethics has been around as long as the study of law, and the two are inextricably connected. Ethics are often split into two approaches: **virtue ethics** and **consequential ethics**. Virtue ethics often look to an outside code to determine what to do. The seminal philosopher in this approach was Immanuel Kant who said that all humans had a duty to act a certain way. He described this duty as the "categorical imperative" (Geyer and Wood, 2012). He said these imperatives are always universal laws that applied to everyone. Categorical imperatives include "to do no harm" and "to tell the truth." In contrast, consequential ethics focus on the outcome of the action. The seminal philosopher in this approach was John Stuart Mill. He argued for utilitarianism, which stated that people should choose to act in a way that served the "greatest good for the greatest number" (Robson, 2013).

The Trolley Problem in the Algorithmic Age

Too often, when deciding how we should act, virtue and consequences conflict. For example, imagine a self-driving car is heading down a road, and someone steps into the road. The AI would be designed to stop. But what if, in doing so, it would likely hurt its own passengers, bystanders, or other drivers by causing a collision with another car. The question is: What does the artificial intelligence decide to do? Does it hurt its own occupants? The bystanders? The other drivers? Or the person who stepped in front of the car? (Pasquale, 2016).

This is certainly a question of ethics. It is actually a modern version of a classic thought experiment in philosophy in which a person has to decide whether to let a runaway trolley kill a group of people or act to divert it, but in doing so, killing one person (Pasquale, 2016). A virtue ethics approach would be to never kill no matter the cost. Therefore, the others would die, but *you* did not do it. Consequential ethics would argue that you kill the one in order to save the many. Of course, in this updated example, the "person" making the decision may not be a person at all.

With this example—and the numerous other examples of issues raised by technology in this book—the question will be: Should there be a policy on this with a dictated punishment if not followed? (see Case Study). In considering these issues, we have to consider our values—personal and social—and how they are implicated. We have to think about the principle to which they would apply: Do you believe in a categorical imperative, utilitarianism, or some other approach? From there we can begin to answer these questions and deliberate with others. From that deliberation, we may change our own thinking or maybe change the others' views on it. When enough of us agree, then our ideas should become a policy or law. Hopefully the law is the optimal solution to the problem.

CASE STUDY
Codifying the Three Law of Robotics?

Science fiction writer Isaac Asimov often focused on robots and artificial intelligence. Most of his work examined how central aspects of humanity, such as morals, ethics, and laws will change because of advancements in artificial intelligence (Asimov, 1984). In his collection of stories titled *I, Robot,* Asimov developed the famous "three laws of robotics":

First Law: A robot may not injure a human being or, through inaction, allow a human being to come to harm.

Second Law: A robot must obey the orders given it by human beings except where such orders would conflict with the First Law.

Third Law: A robot must protect its own existence as long as such protection does not conflict with the First or Second Laws. (Asimov, 1950, p. 40)

Asimov used these laws throughout his works, and other science fiction authors have also adopted them. They became so significant that they have even shaped our real-life philosophical debates on the ethics of AI and how we should advance with its development (Anderson, 2017).

But Asimov's three laws are not foolproof. His work focused on how AI's actions, even when dictated by a well-reasoned law, could lead to unintended consequences. For example, the original three laws implied that a robot could "allow" an action that could hurt a human. So, Asimov had to add "through inaction" to the first law. But robots could still hurt humans, if they were not made aware of the harm they are doing. The laws also do not define harm: Is it only physical harm, or would it include emotional and psychological harms? Then there could be robots that define "humans" as being only from a certain race, age, or gender. Finally, if robots evolved to the point in which they have adopted a sense of being, they might not have to follow the rules at all.

So, Asimov created a fourth law to cover these concerns called Zeroth Law: "A robot may not harm humanity, or, by inaction, allow humanity to come to harm" (Asimov, 1985, p. 353).

This law dictated that robots must protect the greater good. In doing so, Asimov invoked a classic philosophical problem. In fulfilling the Zeroth Law, would the robot have to violate the First Law if killing a human would block humanity from harm? It seems that the advanced AI of the distant future will still be dealing with the fundamental debates from ancient human philosophy.

Discussion Questions

1. Should government adopt the Three Law of Robotics proactively in preparation for the development of advanced AI? Why or why not?

2. Do we already have similar laws that dictate to how humans should treat each other? Are these laws effective?

3. Do the Three Laws of Robotics go far enough? Why? If not, what is missing and needs to be added?

CHAPTER 2

Overview of American Law and Courts

A new video game sparked quite the controversy in the 1970s. As the subheading of a *New York Times* article asked, was it a "cartoon or morbid?" (New York Times News Service, 1976, p. A1). The objective of this game was to run over as many "pedestrians" as one could. The player was not only rewarded with points, but had the added joy of hearing the victims let out a shriek while they laid dying. A non-profit group concerned about consumer safety described that game as "sick, sick, sick." A behavioral psychologist warned: "In this game a player takes the first step to creating violence. The player in no longer just a spectator. He's an actor in the process" (Blumenthal, 1976, p. 12).

The game was called *Death Race*. The arcade-style game was created in 1976 with the primitive pixel graphics of the era. Initially it had a limited release, but the excessive negative attention around it caused sales to skyrocket (Blumenthal, 1976). But in short time the press attention was too much, and the manufacturers pulled the game off the market.

Death Race eventually faded into history, but over the next 4 decades, the social panic over the effect of violent video games was repeated time and time again with games like *Mortal Kombat, Doom,* and the *Grand Theft Auto* series. But it wasn't until the late 1990s that video game manufacturers started facing lawsuits claiming that their products incited violence. After the horrific shooting at Columbine High School in 1999, legislatures across the nation started crafting laws banning the sales of video games to minors. But with little evidence that video games caused violence, courts overturned these laws as unconstitutional. Finally, in 2011, the U.S. Supreme Court held that video games are a form of protected free speech and cannot be regulated differently than other media like books and movies that came before it (*Brown v. Entertainment Merchants Association,* 2011).

In the end, it took 35 years after the social panic around the game of *Death Race* before the legal question of regulating violence in video games was settled. But, in those decades, technology did not stop and wait for the law to catch up. It kept moving at a faster and faster rate. In that time, online gaming, mobile gaming, connected gaming, streaming, and virtual reality all changed the industry. The changes in the technology created even more issues, many of which the law has yet to address.

Why is the law so slow? Well, there are some good reasons. We would not want changes in the law to be reactionary. It should change based on sound reasoning and debate. Legislation must also go through the political system. It starts as policy proposals that are debated. If passed and signed into law, the executive branch will have to enforce them. Courts can then hear disputes in the law. Along the way, the original policy can change as it is interpreted and implemented, hopefully evolving so that it is better at solving the problem it was meant to solve.

This chapter examines the foundation of law in the United States. First, it discusses the purpose and ideals of law and the shortcomings that often occur. Next, it outlines the process of lawmaking—from creation to implementation—and the impact of social norms on the process.

The Purpose and Ideals of Law

We come across many laws in our lives—traffic violations, consumer protection, contracts, property law, and narcotics law to name a few. We often learn about these rules in school or from our parents. Sometimes, we only learn about rules by breaking them. If we violate a rule—like speeding—we are often upset if we get caught. But ultimately, we pay the fine and move on with our lives.

Sometimes we find a rule to be fundamentally unfair. We will certainly complain about it. We may even question the law: When was this law passed? Why is this the law? What is the point of it? Yet, most of the time, after a few days, we pay the fine or stop the action, but rarely do we act to change the law.

But the laws of our nation are the result of a process. They did not start out as law—they started out as a policy or proposal to solve a perceived problem. For example, property law started because private individuals who owned land needed to know where their borders were and what they could do with their property. The general principles of property law have now been in place for thousands of years. U.S. property law was mostly adopted from English **common law** of the middle ages (Robbins Collection, 2010).

This type of **black letter law,** or undisputed and longstanding principles of law, is so entrenched that we rarely ever question the wisdom of these laws. Thus, we fail to examine the genesis of the laws—the problems that arose, the policy proposals, and the heated debates surrounding them. For example, in 2009, the U.S. Congress debated a health care bill that was highly contentious. Republicans disagreed strongly with the law, but the Democratic majority was able to pass it. When Republicans regained control of the federal government in 2016, they attempted to repeal it, but were unsuccessful, because once something is the law and it benefits many constituents, it is very difficult to go back and take it away (Godfrey, 2017).

Policy debates are often painted as being bipolar—Democrat versus Republic, liberal versus conservative, labor versus corporations, and so on. But even these parties, which seem like unified organizations, are made up of many coalitions. Democrats often include environmentalists, civil libertarians, and labor unions. Republicans often include evangelicals, corporate leaders, and farmers (Bacon, 2018). These myriad interests come to the table with different knowledge, experiences, beliefs, and values, even when they belong to the same political party.

Ideally, the law should reflect some consensus among these disparate interests. The final law that is put in place should be a solution to a problem. But it should also reflect what the public believed to be the most workable solution. In doing so, the law should reflect the public's beliefs and values. For example, drug laws were passed because of the perceived issue of drug abuse and its social costs. But it also reflected a belief at the time that using drugs was morally wrong and should not be tolerated in society (of course, this national belief differs depending on the drug, from caffeine to alcohol to marijuana to heroin). Thus, as we consider applying old laws to new problems we should consider their origin—the time, place, and the values at the time of their creation—and whether we still hold these values.

An ideal law should identify a problem and then offer a solution that will be effective. A law should be created through rigorous research followed by a deliberation of the legislative body. It should use language that is clear and precise. Instead, we often get laws that are vague or ambiguous. Sometimes laws are overly technical and filled with legalese, thereby making them burdensome.

But vague laws and technicalities are sometimes required, so the executive branch can have some leeway in applying their expertise. For example, the federal communication acts are very broad and allow the FCC to apply the technicalities. But sometimes vagueness and ambiguity are a political tool, so both parties can claim victory through the passage of the law.

Sometimes, in trying to solve a problem, a law goes too far, and other times it does not go far enough. The latter is particularly worrisome when a law regulates speech, as it may outlaw otherwise protected speech in order to stop some unwanted speech. In these cases, the U.S. Supreme Court may overturn a law that prohibits speech based on it being too broad or vague (Rienzi & Buck, 2002). For example, the Court overturned a law that banned production of videos depicting animal torture. The Court held that the law was overbroad because it would also bar animal rights groups from doing an expose on criminal abuse of animals (*U.S. v. Stevens,* 2010).

Finally, some laws are a reaction to a social fear, such as a tragedy or crisis. For example, the USA Patriot Act was passed shortly after 9/11 and gave the government sweeping powers to fight terrorism. But, in doing so, the law also allowed the government to circumvent our constitutional rights (Khalil, 2005). Either way, laws hastily created as a reaction to a crisis usually do not turn out to be a sound solution to a real problem.

Overview of U.S. Law

Rulemaking Bodies

In the United States, there are numerous sources of law. All three branches of government create rules—legislature write statutes, executive agencies write regulations and courts create **legal tests,** or approaches to settling legal questions. Then the federal government, all 50 states, and D.C., each have their own systems with three branches making rules. Also, within states, there are counties and cities making their own rules. However, **preemption** requires that local ordinances not violate state law and state law not violate federal law. This results in thousands of laws that govern our everyday lives.

The United States is a representative democracy. We vote in politicians who work in the halls of the legislature to pass laws to solve problems at the local, state, and national level. In classic political theory, there is a separation of powers, meaning each branch of government has a certain authority that the other branches cannot exercise. The **legislative branch** passes the law (e.g., U.S. Congress or state legislatures). The **executive branch** is supposed to enforce the law. This branch includes the chief executive (e.g., president or governor), and executive agencies (e.g., FCC, FDA, FAA). The **judicial branch** (e.g., U.S. Supreme Court, federal, state, and local courts) is supposed to only interpret the law.

In the 20th century, U.S. society became larger and more complex. As a result, Congress found that it had neither the vast knowledge needed to regulate many industries nor could it spend the requisite time needed to pass the specific rules in different areas of industry (Presttito 2007). Thus, Congress passed enabling statutes, which created and gave authority to agencies in the executive branch (and state legislatures followed suit). For example, Congress created the Federal Aviation Administration, which makes countless regulations for the airline industry. Today, for most industries, the myriad regulations they are required to follow come from these executive agencies.

But these agencies not only pass rules, they also enforce those rules. Moreover, when an agency enforces a rule, it can also act as a judiciary by holding hearings about violations. Any decision made by the agency can be appealed to a court. But courts often give deference to agencies and uphold decisions so long as they are not *arbitrary or capricious* (Virelli III, 2014). This is an example of the **checks and balances** written into the U.S. constitution.

Sources of Laws

The laws we must follow come from several different sources. In the United States, the Constitution is the highest law of the land. If any other laws violate the Constitution, then they must be overturned. The Constitution allows the president to sign treaties with other nations, and they become law if ratified by the Senate. But, if a treaty agreement violates the Constitution, then it will be declared null and void (*Bond v. United States,* 2011). The U.S. Constitution established principles like federalism, separation of powers, civil liberties, and equal protection. But, for the most part, the U.S. Constitution does not give detail in these areas. Instead, it was left open to some interpretation and ability to adapt, including having a system to amend it. Thus, much of the law is filled in with legislative acts and judicial interpretations.

Much of early U.S. law was adopted directly from England. Some of these laws were statutes that existed. As in the case of copyright law, the United States adopted the Statute of Anne of 1710. But much of English law was **common law**, which is law that was passed down through cases as dictated by judges, such as defamation law. This common law became precedent for courts to use in future cases.

Today, the U.S. judiciary is still rooted in common law, and it is most often seen in constitutional law cases. However, much of U.S. common law has been codified into statutes. For example, libel law, which developed over centuries, is now codified in each of the 50 states and although they all started from the same common law, the 50 state statutes have minor variations.

There are two main classifications of law: criminal and civil. Courts hear both types of cases, but there are differences. **Criminal law** is when the government brings a case against a defendant for committing a crime. The punishment may include fines and/or jail time. In these cases, many civil rights kick in such as a right to a speedy trial, right to an attorney, and right to a jury trial. In criminal court, a defendant can be found guilty or not guilty, and the burden of proof is on the government to prove the case **beyond a reasonable doubt**. If a defendant is found guilty, then a judge imposes a fine or jail sentence (there are guidelines for sentences, sometimes they are mandated, as with sex offenders).

Civil law cases have one party suing another party (this can be individuals, corporations, and even the government). In these cases, the plaintiff is seeking a monetary award. There is a right to a fair proceeding, but there are fewer civil liberties invoked. For example, there is no right to a speedy trial. Also, a judge or jury will decide if a defendant is liable, and the burden of proof for the plaintiff is at least a **preponderance of evidence** (greater than 50%). Finally, the jury or judge will decide the award (even though the plaintiff often asks for an amount).

Criminal defendants have a right to a speedy trial. Thus, those cases have priority over civil cases on a judge's docket. Civil cases take a long time before they are even heard. Parties may try other means to resolve the issue such as **alternative dispute resolutions** (e.g., arbitration) or agreeing to settle before trial. In fact, many companies will choose a settlement over a trial to save on time and the cost of attorneys (the settlement is not made public, and it not a legal admittance of liability, although it sometimes is seen to be in the court of public opinion). The result is that 97% of civil suits that are filed never make it to a trial (Barkai et al., 2006). Although criminal cases get preference, most of those do not go to trial either. About 90% of defendants take a plea deal, usually with the promise of a shorter sentence if they do (Del Valle, 2017).

Statutes are the laws written by legislatures. These are codified laws that often give definitions, punishments, and limitations. The next level of law is **administrative rules**. These are the laws passed by executive agencies, such as the FCC's indecency rules and the FAA's rules for drones. Finally, there are **executive orders**. These are often declarations by the President, which give direction to agencies. Most go unnoticed, but some can have great effect. Presidents may sign executive orders to get an agenda passed without going to Congress, although legislative actions or court decisions can reverse the order. The most infamous executive order was FDR's internment of over 100,000 Japanese Americans during WWII, which the U.S. Supreme Court upheld at the time (*Korematsu v. United States*, 1944). The U.S. Congress officially apologized for the action in the early 1980s. It took until 2018 for the U.S. Supreme Court to note that the case was wrongly decided (see *Trump v. Hawaii*, 2018).

Hierarchy of Law

U.S. Constitution: An original agreement between the states outlining the powers of the federal government

Treaties: An agreement between the United States and another nation

Statutes: Codified laws passed by U.S. Congress and state legislatures

Administrative Rules: Codified rules passed by federal and state agencies per powers granted by legislatures

Executive Orders: Rules passed by the U.S. president or governors to give direction to federal and state agencies.

Overview of the Judicial Branch

Right Person, Right Place, Right Time

Since the 1980s, there has been a move to reform our judicial system based on common belief that we are a judicious society and that everybody is suing everybody for frivolous reasons. Cases like the multimillion-dollar jury awards against McDonalds for serving hot coffee are given as prime examples of what is wrong with the system (Lopez, 2016). But the perception is not accurate. People cannot sue anybody, anywhere, anytime for any reason.

To begin, one must have **standing**, meaning that the plaintiff must have suffered an injury. For example, in *Ruccho v. Common Cause* (2019), the U.S. Supreme Court held that the political parties could not sue for gerrymandering, because they had not suffered a direct injury (*Gill v. Whitford*, 2017). Next, the injury must have occurred for someone to be able to bring a lawsuit. If it is too early, it said not to be **ripe**. In 2010, state attorneys general sued the Obama Administration to stop the Affordable Care Act. But the act had not gone into effect yet, so they could not sue (Kumar & Aizenman, 2011). Sometimes plaintiffs can be too late; these cases are referred to as being **moot**. This has happened in cases in which the press sues the government to gain access to the frontlines of a war, but by the time they sue, the war is over (*Nation Magazine v. U.S. Dept. of Defense*, 1991).

A party also cannot be sued just anywhere. This is a complex subject to which entire law school courses are dedicated. But the shorthand is that you can generally sue in the defendant's home jurisdiction or where they have contacts (NOLO, n.d.). Finally, you cannot sue for any reason. The plaintiff must have an injury needing redress. There must be some proof of this. In filing the case, a judge can review it before it moves forward. If there is no case—even assuming all the facts are true—then the case can be dismissed. This is called a **summary judgment**. If a lawyer brings too many frivolous cases, the person can also be punished to the point of being disbarred.

But many cases do go to court and are heard by a judge or jury. Sometimes, the plaintiff is awarded a large of sum of money for what seems to be a frivolous set of facts. But this is often a function of media reporting. First, reports on a case are often reduced to a headline that does not reflect the evidence a jury hears. Second, the news stories will focus on the large amount of money awarded in the trial. However, those numbers are often reduced on appeal, which are under reported. For example, in the McDonald's 'hot coffee' case, an appeals court reduced the award from $2.8 million to $600,000 (Lopez, 2016).

U.S. courts are an adversarial system. The two parties make arguments, and either one person (a judge) or a group of people (a jury) decides who made the better argument. Though we do believe in ideals—such as truth and justice, and fairness—ultimately, it is the party who had the better argument who wins. Judges are supposed to ensure a fair proceeding, including an unbiased jury, a chance to see all evidence, and question all witnesses to name a few. But that does not mean that the parties are guaranteed the best attorneys to make the best arguments or that the judge and juries seek to find all the evidence. Sometimes, it is simply who ever has the better attorneys wins.

The U.S. Supreme Court

The classic definition of the judicial branch is that it interprets the law. This means that many courts must wait for cases to come to them, and for the U.S. Supreme Court this can take a long time. Moreover, the chance that any one case will get to the Court is quite low. The U.S. Supreme Court has very limited original jurisdiction as most cases reach it only after lengthy appeals. The Court hears only about 70 cases a year, granting less than 6% of appeals (Scotusblog, n.d.). It will usually accept a case if there is disagreement among the lower courts on an issue—often due to a lack of clarity from the high court on the issue. This sometimes happens as technology changes and previous law does not fit well in the new environment. For example, the FCC indecency rules have been around since the 1930s. They were challenged in the 1970s as a violation of free speech. But the U.S. Supreme Court upheld the rules because the original justification of the rules—scarcity of airwaves and pervasiveness of the medium—still held true (*Federal Communications Commission v. Pacifica Foundation*, 1978). But in the late 2000s, the broadcast networks once again challenged the rules believing that the media environment had changed drastically enough to makes the rules moot. It seemed like an opportunity for constitutional law to change with the times

But in *Fox v. FCC* (2012), the U.S. Supreme Court refused to answer the question of the constitutionality of the indecency rules. In doing so, it exemplified two main principles in our legal system. First, it is built on **precedent** or previous decisions. In looking to make a decision, lawyers argue previous case law and justices cite them in their opinions. Second, the U.S. Supreme Court does not like to make drastic changes to the precedent and often aims to limit the effect of the law (Adler, 2015). Although there are historic exceptions—such as *Brown v. Board of Education* (1954) or *Citizens United v. FEC* (2010)—these seismic shifts in the law have been rare (Adler, 2015).

End of Stare Decisis?

Stare Decicis is a latin term for "to stand by things decided." It is an important principle in the American legal system rooted in common law. Courts and lawyers who argue before them must look at precedent—rules from previous decisions—in order to make arguments in the current case. When a case challenges a precedent, courts have some choices about how to proceed. They can accept the precedent and apply it as it is—often reinforcing it. They can modify it or update the precedent for new circumstances (facts, technology, time, etc.). They can distinguish the single case before them as only applying to the particular facts of the case, but not modifying precedent.

Finally, courts have the ability to reverse precedent, thus creating a new precedent. But in the past, courts have been reluctant to do so as it violates the principle of stare decisis. In fact, it can cause upheaval throughout the entire legal system as the foundation that the law and cases were built upon are no longer. Recently, the U.S. Supreme Court has become more willing to overturn Constitutional precedent, such as limits on corporate campaign contributions, providing same-sex marriage protections, and the barring requirements that union members had to pay dues. Justices have begun to openly questions the wisdom of following precedent if they believe it to be wrong.

Constitutional law has been evolving for more than 200 years. But if the Court is more willing to overturn precedent, then the evolution will no longer be slow. In a few years, the Constitutional principles we learn today may not be the same.

See Root, D (2020, January 16). *Precedent matters at the Supreme Court—until it doesn't*. Reason. https://reason.com/2020/01/16/precedent-matters-at-the-supreme-court-until-it-doesnt/

If the U.S. Supreme Court grants a review of a case, it will then receive written briefs from the parties as well as their supporters (called **Amicus Briefs**). Then the Court will hear oral arguments from each side (30 minutes each). But the oral arguments are usually less important than the written briefs (Liptak, 2012). The justices spend months on the written briefs and thinking about the case. The oral arguments are often more about the justices trying to convince other justices, especially a swing vote.

Within a few days after the oral arguments, the justices conference and take a preliminary vote. If the chief justice is in this majority, then s/he will assign the author to write the opinion. If the chief justice is not, then the longest serving member in the majority will decide. This is an important step as the assigner can get a swing vote to join with the promise of authorship. Then the justices take months to write the opinion, which they circulate among each other. There is often some negotiating in this process. Justices decide if they will write their own opinion or join another (see *But You Lost?* text box). Sometimes justices will switch their vote if they find an opinion compelling (Wickman, 2012).

But You Lost?
The Reason U.S. Supreme Court Justices Write Dissents.

There are several types of opinions written by U.S. Supreme Court justices. The first one that appears in every case is the majority opinion. This opinion is the one joined by the most members of the court and reflects their views. Justices may also write concurrences. These are opinions that agree with the outcome of the majority, but not for the same reasons. Sometime the entire court puts out one opinion, either a Per Curiam opinion or a Memorandum Order. Both reflect the decision of the entire court, but a Per Curiam will explain the reasoning, whereas a Memorandum has only a vote and no opinion.

When the court's vote is split, the justices who disagree will write a dissent. The dissent comes after the majority opinion and concurrences. (There are also some opinions that that are concurrence/dissent in part.) The dissenting opinion reflects the view of those who disagree with the outcome in the majority. It can be as long or longer than the majority opinion. For example, in his dissenting opinion in *Citizens United v. FEC* (2010), Justice John Paul Stevens wrote a 90-page dissent (it was his last opinion before he retired). But the views of dissenting judges did not win the day. It was not the precedent. So, why write an opinion at all—who cares?

There is a practical reason for dissents that goes beyond ego and hubris. Obviously, the justices put a lot of thought and deliberation into the opinion. The dissents often express concern about the direction of the law and give warnings. They also can also be a roadmap for the future in hopes that the law will change. The most famous example of this was Justice John Marshall Harlan in the case of *Plessy v. Ferguson* (1896) which constitutionalized "separate but equal." His dissent was the undergirding of the majority opinion in *Brown v. Board of Education* (1955), which overturned *Plessy*.

See Varsave, N. (2019). The role of dissents in the formation of precedent. *Duke Journal of Constitutional Law & Public Policy, 14,* 286–342.

The U.S. Supreme Court is made of nine justices total with eight associate justices and one chief justice. They are chosen by the president and confirmed by the U.S. Senate. Once they are confirmed, they have a lifetime appointment. Justices leave office only if they choose to retire, die in office, or are removed by impeachment, which is rare (Culhane, 2018).

The lifetime appointments are unique in U.S. government. U.S. representatives serve for 2 years and U.S. senators serve 6 years—though there are no term limits. The U.S. president can serve up to two 4-year terms. Thus, they are often at the whims of the political climate. Though incumbency is quite high, the control of Congress often shifts around once every 4 to 8 years, and often it is to the opposite party of the president (Gill, n.d.). But the federal courts are supposed to be immune from the partisan shifts of the other two branches, ideally remaining neutral arbiters.

The Court is supposed to be above politics. But, of course, in practice this may not be the case. The justices are nominated by the president because that person fits a judicial philosophy that follows the partisanship of the president. Over the last 40 years, **originalism** has been connected to Republicans and the idea of a **living constitution** has been connected to Democrats (Shapiro, 2009). Of course, these principled approaches tend to be trumped by partisanship. Justice Scalia who may be the best-known originalist was also known to create a version of past events that best fit his interpretation of what a law should be (Politico, 2018). Because of this, the Court has been viewed as becoming more partisan, which has hurt its standing with the public, although it is still the most respected of the three branches (Thomsen-DeVeaux & Roeder, 2018). Chief Justice Roberts has tried to create an image of the Court as being less political (often to the dismay of the party that nominated him). But the reality is the Court has always been partisan and sometimes hyper-partisan; it is just that today people may be more aware of it (Pritchard, 2018).

Interpretations of Constitution

Textualist: Relies strictly on the words of the law

Originalist: Relies on the meaning of the law at the time of the passing, including text, drafts, floor debates, etc.

Living Constitution: Relies on the above but also believes that the law has to change with time

CASE STUDY
Laws of Technophobia?

The U.S. Supreme Court has had a long history of being weary of technology. We are in the second decade of the 21st century, and the Court still does not allow cameras in the courtroom (even when it is not in session). When it comes to in-house communication, the Court still prefers paper over email—a technology that has been readily available for over 30 years. In a 2014 case about police searches of cell phones, Justice Samuel Alito asked if the police could get personal information someone might be carrying on a "compact disc" (Thomsen-DeVeaux, 2018). In 2020, due to COVID-19, the Court was forced to meet through teleconferencing and for the first time, the general public was allowed to listen to oral arguments live (Barnes, 2020).

The U.S. Supreme Court is not alone in its unfamiliarity with current technology. In a 2019 Democratic Primary debate, Joe Biden told parents to make sure to have the radio on and to "play the record player at night" (Beaumont and Price, 2019). During Congressional hearings on Facebook's use of people's data, a Republican senator fumbled: "Do you track devices that an individual who uses Facebook has that is connected to the device that they use for their Facebook connection, but not necessarily connected to Facebook?" But another senator was more to the point: "What was Facemash and is it still up and running?" (Dunaway, 2018).

This ambivalence toward technology is a concern. As Justice Kagan, who is in her early 60s (10 years younger than the average age of the nine justices) commented: "The justices are not necessarily the most technologically sophisticated people ... [this may] sound quaint and endearing, until you remember that these are the people charged with interpreting the law of the land on issues like online privacy and digital surveillance" (Oremus, 2013, para. 2).

Our legal system is based on looking backwards and using precedents from cases that sometimes date back centuries. The courts look for analogies from technology of the past in order to make a legal precedent apply. For example, when examining privacy issues with iPhones, they will look at privacy cases dealing with landlines and pay phone booths. If the court is applying originalism, then it creates analogies like the one made by Justice Scalia comparing the police using GPS trackers to a British officer jumping into the back of a carriage driven by a colonist (Thomsen-DeVeaux, 2018).

The U.S. Supreme Court also has to wait for cases to come to it, and this can sometimes take up to a decade. In that time, technology can change rapidly, but constitutional protections may not change with it. The hope is the legislatures may answer the call and solve the problems. But currently, the U.S. Congress is in gridlock, and major changes in the law are rare. The last major overhaul to U.S. telecommunications law came in 1996 and a lot has changed in the world of media since then.

Discussion Questions

1. Does the law move too slowly when it comes to the issue of technology? Why or why not?

2. Are there concerns if the law reacted too quickly to each new big thing in technology?

3. Should lawmakers and judges be expected to be well-versed in the technology they regulate? If so, to what degree?

4. What responsibility do younger people have when it comes to making sure that technology is properly regulated?

CHAPTER 3

Censorship of Speech

C hildren learn from watching adults and mimicking their behavior. This is how we all came to learn language. This approach of social learning is now being used to program artificial intelligence, allowing it to learn language from listening to humans. From this surveillance, AI will be able to interact with us. It will be as if we were talking to another human being. But we must ask ourselves: Do we really want AI to speak like we do?

For example, we know all too well that online communication is filled with offensive hate speech. When Microsoft's chatbot Tay learned to speak by following humans' interactions online, "it turned into a racist, pro-Hitler troll with a penchant for conspiracy theories" (Johnston, 2017, para. 12). Microsoft's follow-up chatbot, Zo, also had issues, referring to Microsoft Windows software as "spyware" and the Koran as "very violent" (Vanian, 2018). Facebook also discovered how offensive speech can infiltrate its AI when its algorithm created an advertiser category called "jew hater" (Coldeway, 2017). Unfortunately, technology that directly copies us will be like us—naturally flawed—sometime reflecting the worst aspects of our humanity.

Hate speech did not start with social media. The issue of whether hate speech should be allowed has been raging for decades. Many nations around the world have laws banning it. In the United States, there have been calls to ban it, but the U.S. Supreme Court has decided to protect most speech, even if it is hurtful. Yet, private companies are free to censor offensive speech on their platforms. Even when offensive speech makes it on to their platforms, it is still subject to scrutiny from other users who can chill speakers through shame and outcry. Most of us would agree that offensive speech should not be promoted. Words can hurt. But one of the problems when it comes to censoring speech is who gets to decide what can and cannot be said? Which words are taboo? When and where can they not be said?

Censorship seems contrary to the ideals espoused in liberal democracies. However, when societal change happens too quickly, such as advancements in technology, they can create fear in people. When social institutions and norms are disrupted, people often turn to the false sense of safety and comfort of authoritarian regimes that promise to get things under control. But this attempt at control usually means suspending our civil liberties such as free speech (Ewing, 2017). When another person's speech is being censored, it seems acceptable. But when our speech is being censored, then we realize the tyranny of censorship. With advancing technology, it is no longer just the government that can censor, because the large conglomerates that own the media platforms can censor through algorithms, often without us knowing it is occurring (Gillespie, 2018).

This chapter examines how advancements in communication technology could affect freedom of expression and how governments and tech companies could censor such speech. First, it examines contemporary law protecting speech and government regulation of speech. Second, the chapter investigates looming issues related to how emerging media might challenge the limits of free speech.

Legal Principles of Free Speech

It is almost cliché to say "free speech" is the most revered right for Americans. Many Americans will respond to criticism of their speech by arguing that it is a free country, which allows them to say whatever they want, whenever they want. Yet, when it comes to others with whom they disagree, then they are more than willing to have the others silenced. This "free speech for me, but not for thee" is a popular interpretation of the law (Hentoff, 1992). But this binary concept of free speech is simply wrong (Richards, 2016).

The truth is that, since the beginning of the United States, people have debated the meaning and extent of free speech, and we still do not have a clear answer. But that is the nature of constitutional law—it evolves with passing generations. The text of the First Amendment to the U.S. Constitution is short and simple. It states that "Congress shall make no law ... abridging the freedom of speech, or of the press" (U.S. Const. amend. I). But very few scholars or jurists have subscribed to an absolutist approach to free speech protections; thus, there have always been some restrictions on speech. Even in the 20th century, when the right has expanded greatly, and it seems that we can say anything we want, there are still several categories of unprotected speech (Bhagwat, 2018).

Generally, the government cannot infringe on political speech unless there is a compelling state interest, such as public safety, and it may not prohibit the speech more than necessary to serve the state interest—courts usually find that the law is not narrowly tailored (*Simon & Schuster v. Crime Victims Board*, 1991). Scholars agree that the Founding Fathers were concerned about protecting political speech and the U.S. Supreme Court has stated that it gets the most protection (*Citizens United v. Federal Election Commission*, 2010). Some scholars argue that the Founding Fathers meant to protect political speech only, not other types of speech such as entertainment or advertising, although the U.S. Supreme Court has not adopted that theory (Bhagwat, 2018). But, over the last 100 years, the Court has allowed for more regulation of non-political speech than it has for political speech.

Prior Restraint

Another agreement among scholars and jurists is that the framers of the U.S. Constitution wanted to stop **prior restraint**—when a government censors speech before it occurs, rather than as a post-publication punishment (Meiklejohn, 1948). The founders of the nation were quite familiar with this as they were victims of censorship under the British Crown. Thus, they wanted to ensure that speech critical of the government would be protected in the new nation (see "Justifying Censorship in Times of Crisis?" text box).

The U.S. Supreme Court has placed a very high bar on when the government is allowed to censor speech (*New York Times Co. v. United States*, 1971). In the early 20th century, the U.S. Supreme Court held that some restrictions on speech, which would be tolerated during times of peace, would not be tolerated during wartime (*Near v. Minnesota*, 1931). Famously, the Court held in 1919 that speech could be punished if it was a "clear and present danger" and gave the oft-cited example of not allowing someone to yell "fire" in a crowded theater (*Schenck v. United States*, 1919). However, in *Abrams v. United States* (1919), Justice Oliver Wendell Holmes, who had written the majority in *Schenck*, dissented. He stated that the Court had perverted the clear and present danger test and argued instead for a free marketplace of ideas approach to free speech.

But, as the federal government attempted time-and-time again to restrict speech for national security reasons, the Court responded by placing limits on the government's ability to censor speech. In 1971, the *New York Times* attempted to publish the Pentagon Papers, the U.S. government's self-study on its 30 years build-up in Vietnam. The government sought to stop the publication, arguing that it would reveal confidential information that would put the nation at risk.

The U.S. Supreme Court ruled that the government could not stop the press's publication of the Pentagon Papers. The Court said for the government to be able to stop publication, there needed to be evidence of "grave and irreparable danger" (*New York Times v. United States*, 1971). Because the Pentagon Papers were historical and discussed policy only, they were a political problem and not a danger to national security.

This "grave and irreparable danger" standard has made it very difficult for the government to stop publication of information, and once information is released it is impossible to punish all of the publishers. The government could decide to go after employees who leak classified information with a punishment of prison. But the government cannot stop someone else from publishing leaked information, unless the publisher was involved in the theft of the information (*Bartnicki v. Vopper*, 2001).

Justifying Censorship in Times of Crisis?

In 1781, the United States won its independence from England. The war was fought to provide the colonists freedom from the Crown, including the ability to speak freely and criticize the government. But within 15 years of winning its independence and passing the Bill of Rights, Congress passed the Alien and Sedition Acts of 1798, which made it illegal to criticize the government. The argument for the law was a fear of revolution sweeping across the young United States, one inspired by the French Revolution.

Throughout U.S. history, the government has used times of crisis to suspend civil liberties. Abraham Lincoln suspended habeas corpus during the civil war, the Espionage Act was passed during WWI, and the Patriot Act was passed after 9/11. Though civil libertarians often protest such laws, the general public often welcomes them because they provide safety and order in otherwise fearful times. But removing civil liberties often opens the door to the tyranny and abuse of power as the checks against it are removed. Thus, it is often left to courts to protect the civil liberties against the seemingly good intentioned laws passed by the legislatures.

See Madison, J. (1788). Federalist No. 51. Federalist Papers. https://billofrightsinstitute.org/founding-documents/primary-source-documents/the-federalist-papers/federalist-papers-no-51/

Time, Place, and Manner Restrictions

Despite the high bar on regulating speech, the government does retain some control. The government can rarely regulate speech based on the message unless it is a category of **unprotected speech** such as obscenity, true threats, or incitement to violence. Courts apply a separate legal test for each category of unprotected speech, which we will discuss throughout the book (*Near v. Minnesota*, 1931). The government cannot regulate protected speech based upon its message or speaker as this is a **content based-regulation**. In order to do this, the government would have to show a compelling state interest and that the law is narrowly tailored so not to block protected speech. Public safety is always a compelling state interest, but there is usually a less restrictive alternative to blocking speech. For example, protests at abortion clinics can disrupt the peace, but instead of stopping the protest, the government can provide buffer zones, barriers, and police (*McCullen v. Coakley*, 2014).

The government can regulate protected speech when it comes to the **time, place, and manner** of the speech. For example, the government cannot restrict a White supremacist group from having a parade based on its message or the speakers (*National Socialist Party of America v. Village of Skokie*, 1977). This would be considered an unconstitutional content-based regulation. But the government could restrict the time of such a parade so that it could not occur at night. The government could not restrict protests on civil rights, but it could regulate if the speakers were amplified through bullhorns (*Ward v. Rock Against Racism*, 1989).

Time and manner restrictions are fairly straight-forward. The more difficult concept is the place restriction. The U.S. Supreme Court has developed a **forum doctrine** used to determine where and how the government can regulate. The forum doctrine provides four types of forums: traditional public, designated public, limited public, and non-public (*Perry Education Association v. Perry Local Educators*, 1983).

A **traditional public forum** is considered to be a government-owned space that has been open to the public immemorial, such as streets and parks. In this type of forum, the government can enforce content-neutral time and manner regulations only. A **designated public forum** is government-owned property that has been opened to the public for expressive purposes. This might be an auditorium or meeting room. The principle issue in these cases is that the government clearly indicates this area be open to expression. Just because expression has occurred on the space does not mean that it is designated, but courts may consider the stated purpose and use of government space. If it is considered a designated public forum, then it will be treated the same as a traditional public forum.

If the government property is not a traditional or designated public forum, then it is considered a **limited public forum** or **non-public forum**. A limited public forum is open to certain groups or types of speech only. In this forum, the government can enforce any regulation so long as it serves a legitimate state interest and the regulation is reasonably related to serving that interest. For example, a classroom is open to students and teachers only to discuss germane academic topics, but incendiary speech may not be allowed. This regulation is reasonable considering the government interest in educating students.

Finally, a non-public forum is government property closed off to public expression, such as inside a prison. In this type of forum, the government can control any speech so long as it serves a reasonable interest, such as order in the prison.

True Threats, Incitement, and Hate Speech

In the U.S., there are several categories of speech that are not protected including defamation (Chapter 4), obscenity (Chapter 7) and copyright infringement (Chapter 8). The U.S. Supreme Court has also recognized two other categories of unprotected speech: true threats and criminal incitement.

The U.S. Supreme Court has defined a threat as "statements where the speaker means to communicate a serious expression of an intent to commit an act of unlawful violence to a particular individual or group of individuals" (*Virginia v. Black*, 2003). **True threats** are illegal, but they are difficult to prosecute. For example, Anthony Elonis was a man whose life had bottomed-out. His wife told him that she was leaving and taking their two children with her. So, Elonis turned to Facebook to express his frustrations.

Initially, he posted a picture of himself at a costume party holding a fake knife to a co-worker's throat. The caption read: "I wish." This led to him being fired from his job. Then he posted a paragraph about his wife saying, "Do you know it's illegal for me to say I want to kill my wife." After a complaint was made, he was visited by a law enforcement officer. He next posted a paragraph, which included, "Took all the strength I had not to turn the bitch ghost. Pull my knife, flick my wrist, and slit her throat." (*Elonis v. United States*, 2017).

Elonis was arrested for making threats. In court, he argued that it was artistic expression as he was an aspiring rap artist and went by the name Tone Dougie, and he often stated on his posts that they were fictitious and therapeutic. A trial court disagreed and found Elonis guilty of making threats. He was sentenced to 44 months in prison.

In reviewing the conviction, the U.S. Supreme Court held that just because others felt threatened was not enough to prove a threat was made. Instead, the government had to prove the defendant *intended* to make a threat. Because it is a criminal prosecution, this meant that the government had to prove this **intent** beyond a reasonable doubt, a difficult standard when proving someone's thoughts. The Court reversed and remanded the case. But on remand, the Third Circuit upheld Elonis's appeal of the conviction (and time served) applying Justice Alito's concurrence that recklessness was enough to be found guilty of a threat. The U.S. Supreme Court refused to hear his second appeal (*Elonis v. United States*, 2017). After all of this, what constitutes a true threat is no clearer.

Another category of unprotected speech is **criminal incitement**. This is when someone attempts to, or does, inspire others to commit a crime (such as violence, rioting, and overthrowing the government). In order for such speech to rise to level of incitement, the government must prove that: 1) The speaker had intent; 2) there was a call for lawless action; and 3) the speech was likely to (or did) cause the lawless action (*Virginia v. Black*, 2003).

But once again, because of the criminal intent element, this crime is difficult to prove. Someone might go on social media and post a message that "we need to start a revolution." Even if someone read it and was inspired and attacked a government facility, it would be difficult to prove that the original poster meant an armed overthrow of the government—the person might have meant revolution through the process of election.

In addition, the element of causation may be even more burdensome for a prosecutor, because the government either has to convince a court that the lawless action would have happened (which requires a judge or jury to be clairvoyant) or, if the lawless action did occur, then the government must prove the speech actually caused the audience to act. This is nearly impossible because of the many intervening variables that can occur between the speech and the criminal action (e.g., time, mental capacity of the actor, physical distance between speech, and crime). Remember, because this is a criminal case, the government must once again prove all the elements beyond a reasonable doubt (Chapter 7 will discuss incitement as a civil tort).

One category of speech that many people think is illegal is **hate speech**. But, in the United States, hate speech is not prohibited; in fact, there is no legal definition. Nonetheless, it is understandably a controversial topic, and people who use offensive speech can be punished by private parties, such as their employers, or they can be publicly humiliated. But the U.S. Supreme Court has been clear that it will rarely allow criminal prosecution of hate speech based solely on the content, no matter how abhorrent the message.

For example, the Court refused to uphold a multimillion-dollar civil judgment against the Westboro Baptist Church—a group who regularly protested at the funerals of fallen soldiers, claiming that God was punishing the United States for acceptance of homosexuality. In the case, Chief Justice Roberts succinctly summarized the Court's approach on offensive speech: "As a Nation we have chosen a different course—to protect even hurtful speech on public issues to ensure that we do not stifle public debate" (*Snyder v. Phelps*, 2011).

The difference between threats/incitement, which is not allowed, and hate speech, which is allowed, is the distinction made between the thought and the action. True threats are prohibited because the defendant intentionally made statements about committing violence. Incitement to violence is prohibited because the defendant intended to cause criminal activity. But the mere utterance of hateful speech is protected, even if the offensive speech was to cause the target to respond with violence, because the speaker did not show an intention of action. Hate speech can be punished only if the speaker had an intent to intimidate because it then becomes a true threat (*Virginia v. Black*, 2003). In fact, the government must protect someone who uses hate speech from an audience's response to shut down that speech. The government must prevent the **heckler's veto**, often through the use of police barricades and protection for the speaker who is spewing hate.

The Birth and Death of Fighting Words?

In 1940, Walter Chaplinsky, a Jehovah's Witness, was preaching in the streets of Rochester, NH. He passed out pamphlets and made comments that organized religion was a racket. This caused a stir among the crowd who began to berate Mr. Chaplinsky. Local officials saw the commotion and decided to intervene by asking Chaplinsky to stop. Chaplinsky became upset and called the city marshal a "damn fascist" and a "God-dammed racketeer." Chaplinsky was then arrested for his offensive outburst.

Chaplinsky challenged the arrest as a violation of his free speech. But the U.S. Supreme Court upheld the conviction claiming that the speech was in an unprotected category called "fighting words." These are words that are so horrible that the mere utterance would cause a breach of the peace. After this case, fighting words became part of U.S. jurisprudence and lexicon.

However, the U.S. Supreme Court never used the category again. Instead, courts have relied upon other categories like incitement and threats and has often protected controversial speakers with concepts such as the heckler's veto. The Court refuses to create a list of words that are so bad that they cannot be spoken. Nonetheless, the doctrine still exists, but the U.S. Supreme Court has never used it.

See *Chaplinsky v. New Hampshire*, 315 U.S. 568 (1942).

See Smolla, D. A. (2009). Words "which by their very utterance inflict injury": The evolving treatment of inherently dangerous speech in free speech law and theory, *Pepperdine Law Review*, 36(2), 317–360. http://digitalcommons.pepperdine.edu/plr/vol36/iss2/4

Virtual Issues in Free Speech and Censorship

1. Should virtual spaces be considered public forums requiring free speech protection?

Currently, most people do not meet their national representatives in person. Many of us do not even get to meet our state or local government representatives. Most of our experiences with politicians come through mediated channels. Furthermore, politicians are able to bypass traditional media filters and speak directly to the electorate through social media.

Citizens do interact with their government every day, and much of the business is still done in person and through paperwork. But governmental adoption of digital technologies has allowed for more and more of government business to take place online. These practices could soon be extended to virtual reality. In these virtual spaces, candidates could meet with voters, and representatives could meet with constituents. Trials and appellate cases could even take place in virtual spaces (Kaufman, 2017).

These "public" spaces would likely be governed by the forum doctrine. But when it comes to virtual spaces, the analysis is not so simple. By definition, newly created spaces cannot be traditional, so they would either be considered designated or limited public forums. When candidates and representatives hold in-person open forums, the events are tightly controlled. Often it is for security reasons, but sometimes it is to remove protesters or to protect against unwanted questions. Attendees to events are often invited and screened (Rowland & Goodman, 2016).

Many politicians have opened up social media accounts to speak to their constituents. But in doing so they have opened a forum that allows for the public to speak directly back without censorship. Several politicians have been sued for blocking citizens from their Twitter account (Roberts, 2019). The most prominent example was when President Trump attempted to block critics from his Twitter account. Although it is a privately-owned forum, a federal court in New York ruled that the president could not do so because he designated it a public forum when he opened the account for official government business (*Knight First Amendment Institute v. Trump*, 2019).

This rule could be extended to any virtual environment that government officials use for official government business; thus, they would not be able to control the content or message of such speech. But the nature of VR space may be different than responses to a Twitter account. If a politician is holding an event open to the public, protestors cannot be censored. However, in a physical space, protestors can be moved away from the central location. This is often done in the name of safety to the government official. If the protests are too disruptive, then the protestors can also be removed. If a VR space replicates a physical space, then the Twitter analogy may not apply. Instead, protestors on VR could be removed just the same as if they were in a physical space. Of course, the politician being protested against would surely welcome it.

2. Should tech companies work with governments that do not protect free speech?

Tech companies are often strong supporters of free speech principles, sometimes including these ideals in their corporate mission statements. For example, Google's mission statement is "to organize the world's information and make it universally accessible and useful" (Google, n.d.). But, when it comes down to application, private actors, including tech companies, are not legally bound by the principles of free speech.

Moreover, internationally, tech companies have to follow the laws within the nation their platforms are accessed. If they do not, they will not be granted access to the large consumer markets. In the U.S., the government cannot stop otherwise protected speech, unless there is a clear showing of a threat to public safety. But in some nations, the government is willing and able to censor its citizens, especially dissidents. So, if tech companies want to operate within these nations, they may have to censor speech.

For example, Google debated whether it would work with the Chinese government and its authoritarian practices in order to access billions of more customers or if it would uphold the principles of free speech. Google has faced criticism in the United States whenever it was willing to censor content in order to appease the Chinese government. In 2010, Google ended its search service in China due to the heavy censorship by the government. But, under a decade later, reports surfaced that Google was working with the Chinese government to return to their markets (Gallagher, 2018).

It can be problematic for international conglomerates when platforms are dispersed throughout many different jurisdictions. Social media companies will often have different versions of a platform depending on the nation in which it is being sold. But, when one nation puts in a minimum standard, it is often easier for a company to place the same rules on all access points rather than having varying rules. For example, when the European Union passed new privacy laws that websites had to follow, tech companies then included these same rules for all U.S. users, even though they were not legally obligated to do so. Of course, the U.S. users have become more concerned about privacy, and many have welcomed the new rules (Tiku, 2018).

However, there are fears that if tech companies put in policies to appease more authoritarian governments, the policies will reverberate and impact users in more democratic nations, especially if those governments find them to be effective with surveillance and social order (Li, 2018). China's social-credit system scores citizens based on many factors including expressive factors such as giving to charity, playing music loudly, playing too many video games, belonging to certain religious groups, and criticizing the government. A person with a low score can be punished by revealing to the public and businesses the score; thus, they are treated differently. It uses AI, IoT and facial recognition technology to collect and assess data. A person with a high social-credit score is often given benefits such as more access to health care, government services, and business services. A similar system could be developed in more democratic countries, but veiled in the terms of venture capitalism, public health, and self-improvement (see Chapter 4) (Coldry & Mejias, 2019).

3. Should tech companies be able to censor speech on their platforms and virtual spaces?

In the early years of the internet, Congress passed Section 230 of the Communications Decency Act (1996) to protect companies from liability for what third parties say on their platforms. It was meant to protect nascent internet companies from costly lawsuits at a time when they could not afford them. Congress' intent was to allow internet companies to regulate content and to be free from liability when they did so (Kosseff, 2019). Instead, since its inception, the law has been used as almost blanket immunity against third party actions (with the exception of copyright infringement and federal crimes).

Many critics argue that Sec. 230 has created an environment of lawlessness as digital companies do not monitor verbal attacks, hate speech, or other offensive speech (Mancini, 2018). But in recent years, tech companies have responded to public criticism and have been more attentive to creating and enforcing censorship rules. Now, social media companies each have their own nebulous policies on acceptable speech, regulating things like indecency, bullying, hate speech and fake news. For example, Facebook removes pictures of breastfeeding for violating it rules of decency (Lapowsky & Levy, 2018). Conservatives argue that social media companies are also purposely censoring right-leaning voices because they believe Silicon Valley has a liberal agenda (Schwartz, 2018).

But it was the 2016 U.S. Presidential campaign and the explosion of misinformation that put the question of responsibility of the tech companies into the public consciousness. Over the last several years, Russian operatives were able to inflame the political divisions in the United States. The Russian groups created fake social media accounts to act as vocal support for opposing political groups. For example, if a police shooting of an unarmed African American occurred, Russian accounts would pose as either Black Lives Matter or All Lives Matter supporters in an attempt to agitate the other side (Clifton, 2018).

The Russian bot campaign on U.S. social media was not unique. Russia has targeted other nations with disinformation campaigns. Iran has used bots to spread anti-Israel propaganda and support for the nuclear agreement. China has been accused of using bots to spread propaganda interfering with Australian and Taiwanese elections (Pierson, 2018). In Malaysia, government-sponsored bots were able to drown-out a social media campaign to help poor voters get to the polls (Shiff, 2018).

The Russian campaign to spread disinformation was not unlike many trolls that litter the social media landscape. However, the difference was that much of this work was from automated bots. According to a federal indictment, the objective was to create "political intensity" in the United States (Apuzzo & LaFranier, 2018). It is near impossible to measure the impact it had on the election, if any, but it certainly stoked the fears of U.S. technological and political vulnerabilities.

Since 2016, social media companies have been working to identify and remove coordinated accounts aiming to interfere with political elections. Foreign efforts to influence elections violate U.S. law (Voting and Elections, 2002), and furthermore, social media sites can dictate their own policies. But, if the accounts are based in the U.S., the companies have to take into consideration that political messages are protected as free speech, a principle they have publicly supported. Social media companies must also consider that fringe political ideas may be read as offensive speech. The companies must decide if they want to be the ones to select which speech to censor or face the possibility that the government will step in and force regulation ("Why Washington," 2018). This can be a difficult tightrope for companies to walk.

In many European nations, hate speech is illegal ("Countering Illegal", 2018), but in the United States, it is not. The difficulty is that much of U.S. communication is through international social networks controlled by large corporations. When working in an international legal mosaic, it is much easier for companies to install a program that survives the most restrictive laws of one nation, knowing that it will work in all. Moreover, because corporations do not need to follow the First Amendment, they can place stricter rules on their own platforms. Sec. 230 of the Communications Decency Act states that sites can filter information anyway they choose without fear of being sued by users. This allows Twitter to permanently ban users, as it has done with several prominent White nationalists and conspiracy theorists ("Twitter Suspensions," n.d.).

Companies also use their own bots to enforce these speech rules. Facebook's optical character recognition system, called Rosetta, can read memes, which can help the company identify hate speech (Matsakis, 2018). However, these bots currently cannot navigate legal nuances or make decisions based on unique contexts. Thus, protected speech is often unnecessarily flagged on social platforms. For example, in 2018, a small newspaper posted sections of the Declaration of Independence verbatim on its Facebook page. One post was blocked by the bots as it referred to "Savage Indians." Under Facebook's policies, this was considered "denigrating speech." The bots were unable to figure out that it was a direct quote from a historical document and that the post was not promoting such language or ideas, although actual people at the company later fixed the error (Kelleher, 2018).

4. **Will threats and incitement be more powerful in VR, requiring more limits on free speech?**

Much like social media platforms today, virtual reality spaces will be owned by private companies. Thus, they will probably operate with similar rules for speech, by regulating offensive speech such as hate speech, obscenity, and harassment. This will likely be a mix of self-regulation along with the requirements of the locality in which it is being accessed. Social media companies currently self-regulate by having users report when they are receiving threats or being harassed. Such incidents are flagged, and users can be removed from the site, and in many cases people are reported to the police.

But in the legal system it can be difficult to prove online threats because of distance in time and space between the speaker and the intended recipient. It is not akin to someone making a threat face-to-face in real time. But VR may be a platform that is somewhere between social media and face-to-face. Moreover, the psychological effect of the speech in VR may be similar to a face-to-face encounter (Kramer, et al., 2019). And if avatars are considered to be an extension of one's identity (see Chapter 8), then the threat may have an actual impact on the person. It may be considered assault, which requires more than speech, but does not require physical contact.

Virtual reality is also a forum for people to assemble. VR platforms are now being used by businesses to bring together a growing mobile workforce that cannot meet in the same physical space (Ngan, 2018). Similarly, multi-player online games allow groups of friends, who may be spread across the world, to meet in a virtual space. In some ways it is more attractive than social media or video conferencing, especially when meeting new people, as avatars can stand in place for the physical person.

But these meeting spaces could also become places for extremists to meet and conspire, just as social media have been used by groups like ISIS to recruit members and inspire so-called "lone wolves" (Leetaru, 2018). VR technology could also be used by such groups for training purposes to simulate war or acts of terror. Whereas the 9/11 hijackers had to take classes at a flight school, in 2018, a ground worker for Alaska Airlines was able to fly off with a plane based on what he described as playing video games (Morris, 2018). With advanced VR technology, fringe groups could train new recruits in an environment that is just as good as the real thing.

The question is whether VR companies will allow such groups to meet at all. If tech companies decide to monitor extremist groups, will the companies then pass on information to authorities such as the FBI, which can then track or infiltrate these groups. After 9/11, tech companies were willing to work with authorities to help monitor extremist groups. But, as whistleblowers exposed, sometimes tech companies were too willing to bypass civil liberties, including monitoring groups who did not pose a threat to national security (Gellman & Portras, 2013).

Nevertheless, even if extremist groups are barred from corporate-owned VR forums, there could still be privately created forums where groups could meet. If accessed through a virtual private network (VPN) and/or the Dark Net, it could be much more difficult for authorities to monitor (Viney, 2016).

CASE STUDY
Human Rights for Artificial Intelligence?

In June 2017, social media were abuzz. There was impending doom as Silicon Valley had gone too far in playing god. The news was that Facebook had to shut down its AI project because the program had created its own unique language. What did the bots say to each other? Were they in the early steps of planning our annihilation and laughing about when they will be in power?

Here was the actual conversation between the two bots:

Bob: "I can can I everything else."

Alice: "Balls have zero to me to me to me to me to me."

The real story was that the language was simply gibberish, and it was not what Facebook was trying to accomplish. However, social media clickbait made it seem as though Facebook had killed the "master switch" in order to prevent the growing concern over the AI evolving beyond our control. But the reality was that the AI was malfunctioning, and the process needed to restart. This social panic points to a significant fear in humans—AI will evolve past our intellect, thus leaving us without control over the very machines we have created (Wilson, 2017).

This fear is not new. It is a trope long used in Hollywood, including movies such as *Terminator* (1988), The Matrix Trilogy, and *Ex Machina* (2014). The popular HBO series *Westworld* (an adaptation of a 1972 book by Michael Crichton) examines a future in which humans can visit a theme park inhabited by robots who are indistinguishable from the human guests. In this park, humans get to live out their fantasies, which are mostly acts that are taboo in the real world such as sex, robbery, and murder. The story hinges upon the question of what happens once the robots break the controls of their human masters and begin to show a semblance of free will.

In these Hollywood creations, most of the robots are unable to have emotional intelligence or sympathy. But there is usually one AI character who seems to be more human than robot, and the audience can relate to this struggle to live in both worlds. Of course, in these stories, ultimately the humans win out through their courage and ability to stick together to preserve the human race. But is this science fiction closer to science or to fiction?

AI is in our homes today, most notably in digital assistants such as Alexa and Siri. Soon these home AI platforms may be embodied in droids that will appear more and more humanlike. The development of these AI artifacts may move from being simply appliances to being more like household pets. Over the last century, we have witnessed the development of "animal rights," a belief that animals should be freed from abuse, killing, and captivity. This "animal rights" movement grew with the domestication of animals—from the owners of cats and dogs and other lovers of animals.

So, it is not unreasonable that a similar development could happen for AI. This would go against the pop culture trope of a revolt by a superior AI that annihilates human existence. Instead, there would need to be a symbiotic movement between humans and the AI seeking rights. In fact, the European

Union is already considering a framework for protection of AI, including a legal definition of AI, a code of ethics for design, and liability for owners. It is laws like this that may be the first step in the next civil rights movement.

Discussion Questions

1. Could a civil rights movement for AI ever develop in our law?

2. If so, what would such a law look like? What rights would society be willing to give to AI artifacts?

3. How would the policy develop? What would be the politics behind it?

4. If AI develops to a point where its intelligence is equal to or surpasses human intelligence, should it be given equal rights such as free speech?

CHAPTER 4

False Speech

I n April 2018, former President Barack Obama released a PSA to warn of the dangers that technology poses. In the video, the former president states that our enemies could make him say anything like Black Panther's nemesis "Killmonger was right" or that President Donald Trump is "a total and complete dip shit." Obama then reveals that he would never say this (in public), but comedian Jordan Peele would, who is then shown impersonating the former president's voice over a digitally edited video (Silverman, 2018). Jordan Peele had produced the video for Buzzfeed to illustrate how **deepfakes** can manipulate people. Digitally edited videos are not new, but as the technology advances, they are becoming more convincing.

This Buzzfeed video used Peele's impersonation, so it was not an exact copy, but other videos may edit together a speaker's past statements or even manipulate sounds to make new words. Although most of the deepfakes on the internet are for entertainment purposes ("Top 10," 2019), governments are very concerned about the manipulative nature of these videos. As disinformation campaigns have been used to seed dissent and chaos through social media, deepfakes could be an even more powerful tool as the visual disinformation would be vastly more difficult to guard against. The simple fact is that, even if many of us question what we read or hear, it is much more difficult for us not to believe what we see.

But it is not just global politics that can be targeted; this editing technology could soon be used against individuals. For example, cyberbullying could become much more vicious if deepfakes are used to destroy reputations of everyday people. Taken to the extreme, AI might be developed to mimic actual persons and spread disinformation in a virtual environment, taking on an alternate life all its own outside the control of the real person. If left unchecked, the only defense for us may be to not believe any information we come across. But, without trust, societies crumble.

This chapter examines how advancements in technology can affect the dissemination of false information and our legal ability to protect our reputations and perceptions of truth. First, it covers contemporary laws regulating false speech and protecting reputations. Second, it investigates issues with emerging technology and the dissemination of false speech.

Legal Principles in False Speech

Defamation Law

The **tort** of defamation seeks to protect plaintiffs against lies that negatively affect their reputation. It allows for plaintiffs to repair their reputation in the public forum of a court. It also punishes the speakers who have spread the lies.

Defamation law is one of the oldest areas of law in the Anglo-American jurisprudence (Garfield, 2011), and some of the original common law is still on the books today. However, one significant difference with the original common law was the burden of proof required to win a case. For centuries, plaintiffs could prevail in a case by simply showing that there was a statement about them that could hurt their reputations (*New York Times v. Sullivan*, 1964). In practice, all the plaintiff really had to do was convince the judge or jury that the statement was offensive. Moreover, the damages were presumed and the burden was on the defendant to prove the statements were true (Lake, 2009).

Currently, to win a libel case, generally a plaintiff must prove: "1) the defendant must publish a defamatory statement; (2) that is false; (3) that is of and concerning the plaintiff; (4) the defendant must have some degree of fault; and (5) the statement must damage the plaintiff" (American Law Institute, 1977, Sec. 558). All plaintiffs must prove that there was a statement of fact about them that injured their reputation. But when it comes to falsity and fault, who has the burden of proof depends upon whether the plaintiff is considered a public figure or not.

U.S. defamation law is codified on the state level with each of the 50 states having a version of it. Although they differ in some respects, the differences are minimal as most have adopted the common law and the constitutional requirements to the law discussed in this chapter.

The terms slander and libel are technically different. Slander is defamatory statements that are spoken, and libel is defamatory statements that are written. In the past, there were legal differences as libel was seen to be more serious as it was thought out, permanent, and meant the person who wrote it was educated. Today, defamatory statements that are published in social media, texts, or videos would all be considered libel. Some courts and legal scholars have argued that the use of different terms of libel and slander is no longer necessary (Marton et al., 2010).

Plaintiff's Elements to Prove Defamation

1. Publication: defendant published a statement

2. Identification: statement was about the plaintiff

3. Defamatory: statement injured the plaintiff's reputation

4. Falsity: the statement was false

5. Fault: the publication was not an innocent mistake

Elements of a Defamation Suit

The first element of **publication** is fairly straight-forward. A plaintiff must show that there was a third person who heard the statement. Though the law uses the word publication. Though the law uses the word publication, the channel of expression does not matter. It could be spoken, written, signed, texted, filmed, etc. As long as the message was communicated, then it is a publication. This element requires only one other person, but for other elements in the suit it is inherent that more people came across the statement.

The second element of **identification** requires that the person(s) who came across the statement would recognize that it was about the plaintiff (American Law Institute, 1977, Sec. 617a). This does not mean that the identification needs to be explicit, like a name or photo. Identification can be shown if it can be reasonably inferred from the totality of the facts. For example, descriptions, such as the plaintiff's address, occupation, height, weight, and tattoos, could be sufficient so long as the audience can identify the plaintiff (*Hart v. Electronic Arts*, 2013). Of course, the audience would have to be familiar with the defendant in order to infer such a description.

Misidentification also rises to the level to defamation. For example, a news outlet writes a story about a suspect named "John Smith." But, because it is a common name, it posts a picture of the wrong "John Smith." For this element, if the audience believes that the defendant was referring to the plaintiff, then it is sufficient. (When it comes to fault, then the reasoning behind the news agency's act would matter).

The third element of injury requires that the statement must put the plaintiff in lower standing or deterred others from associating with the person (American Law Institute, 1977, Sec. 559). At one time, there was a category of **libel per se**—words that were so bad that they were automatically considered to be defamatory. This included accusations of criminal behavior, scrupulous morals, or infectious disease (Rosini, 1991). Today there are almost no words that are automatically defamatory as language can be ambiguous, figurative and hyperbolic. Courts now consider the statements in the context of the speaker, the audience, and the culture—referred to as **libel per quod**. For example, discussions on social media and cable news shows are filled with incendiary language. But the custom in these media is for exaggeration, such as calling their political opponents liars, cons, or even terrorists. But most of the audience knows that these are not literal uses of the word (Steenson, 2014).

A statement can be defamatory, but a plaintiff will not prevail in the case without showing an actual injury to his or her reputation (*Gertz v. Welch*, 1974). In relief, a plaintiff can request a retraction of the statement, an injunction against further publication, or monetary damages (American Law Institute, 1977, Sec. 568). Any direct injury that can be quantified, such as a loss of a job or customer, can be recovered as **compensatory damages**. Moreover, a jury can decide to punish the defendant and send a message to anyone considering defaming another. These **punitive damages** are usually the large sums awarded in a jury trial. But, in order to win punitive damages on a statement regarding a matter of public concern, a plaintiff would need to show that the defendant knew they were lying (see below).

Constitutional Protections

The fourth and fifth elements of libel implicate constitutional issues. Prior to U.S. Supreme Court decisions in the 1960s and 1970s, common law defamation often applied **strict liability** on the defendant; thus, they were liable even if was a simple mistake. Also, the defendant had the burden of proof to show that the statement was true.

But, in the seminal case of *New York Times v. Sullivan* (1964), the U.S. Supreme Court added a **fault standard** to U.S. libel law. The Court stated that the First Amendment requires "breathing space" in the discussion of public affairs (*New York Times v. Sullivan*, 1964). As a result, false statements will sometimes be traded in the public sphere, and defendants cannot be burdened with strict liability when discussing politics.

Initially, the Court created an **actual malice** standard when public officials sue for defamation coming from statements on matters of public concern.

In order to win such a case, the plaintiff would have to prove that the defendant made the statements "with knowledge that it was false or with reckless disregard of whether it was false or not" (*New York Times v. Sullivan*, 1964).

In later cases, the Court extended this fault standard to any plaintiff who is a public figure. There are two categories of public-person plaintiffs. The first is **all-purpose public figures**—people who can defend themselves in the public realm. This is usually public officials and celebrities (*Gertz v. Robert Welch, Inc.*, 1974). But this is not absolute. For example, not all public officials would be all-purpose public figures. Elected officials would count, but only if the statement pertains to their jobs. Though, in contemporary politics it seems like all aspects of a candidate's life are for consideration for their jobs. As far as celebrities, it is a matter of their power to defend themselves through media channels. Of course, in the digital era, everyone has access to social media and can defend themselves (O'Connor, 2011).

The second category of public-person plaintiff is the **limited-purpose public figure** plaintiff. The U.S. Supreme Court considers a limited-purpose public figure plaintiff to be someone who has "thrust themselves to the forefront of a controversy" (*Gertz v. Robert Welch, Inc.*, 1974, p. 344), but courts have had difficulty defining this clearly. An example might be the students who attended a high school where a school shooting occurred and who went on a media platform to take a side on the political issue of gun control. If these students sued someone for defamatory comment based on their views on gun control, then would likely be considered public figures. But if the defamatory comment was based on a different issue or just a personal attack, then the students would be considered private persons.

Moreover, the person must have put him or herself in the spotlight voluntarily. If it was not their own choice, for example, a job required them to speak on the issue, then they may not be considered a limited-purpose public figure. Also, being defamed does not make a plaintiff a public figure, even if they received media coverage. They must have been a public figure before the defamation.

Finally, a few courts have recognized a limited category of the **involuntary limited-purpose public figure**. These plaintiffs do not have to thrust themselves into a controversy. Instead the controversy is of such great public importance that they automatically become public figures and would have to prove actual malice (Usman, 2014). This concept was described by the U.S. Supreme Court (*Gertz v. Robert Welch, Inc.*, 1974), but is so rare that there is no consistent way to determine who would be one (Kluft, 2014).

If the plaintiff is not one of the public figures mentioned above, then they are considered a private person plaintiff. In most states, these plaintiffs must show only at least negligence or that the defendant did not take due care in publishing the statement (States can give more free speech protections and require all plaintiffs to prove actual malice). For example, if the truth could have been ascertained with some research—like a criminal record—then it would have been negligent to make the statement without doing so.

The final element of whether the statement is libelous is **falsity**. If it is true, then it is not libelous (see Defenses). However, under the common law, the plaintiff did not have to prove it was false in order to win the case. Today, this element hinges upon the type of plaintiff. Public figure plaintiffs will have to prove falsity, while private persons plaintiffs usually do not.

Proving a Negative?

In any court case, the burden of proof is important. The plaintiff most often has it, but it can shift. Moreover, the level of proof—such as "beyond a reasonable doubt" versus "preponderance of evidence"—can change the chances of who prevails. In a libel case, the requirement of falsity shifts based on the type of plaintiff, and this is an important distinction as proving something to be true or false can be quite difficult. Proving truth may be easier—so long as you have proof. But how do you prove abstract concepts like whether you love someone or believe in a certain religion?

Falsity is even more difficult to prove. How do you prove that you do not do drugs or that you have never stolen? All you can show is that you have never been caught. Furthermore, to prove a statement to be true or false sometimes means divulging other information you do not want public. What if a plaintiff could prove that accusations of an affair were not true, but in doing so had to reveal other aspects of his sexuality that he did not want revealed? What if a person has an alibi to an accusation of a crime, but the alibi is an even worse crime? The idea behind libel law is it allows people to scream from the mountaintops in order to exonerate themselves. But the truth is, it is not always that easy.

Defenses to Defamation

The plaintiff must prove all five elements to win a defamation case. So, the defense would seek to attack any one of those elements—publication, identification, and injury. The defendant would also try to show that the plaintiff was a public figure, thus shifting the burden onto the plaintiff to prove falsity as well as actual malice.

But even if the plaintiff proves all the elements, defendants still have defenses available to them. The ultimate defense is truth (*New York Times v. Sullivan*, 1964). If the defense can prove that the statement is true, then there is no lawsuit. Also, libel defendants do not have to be perfect; they will be protected so long as the statement was substantially true. The U.S. Supreme

Court has allowed for misquotes and even deliberately edited interviews to be protected, as long as they do not materially alter the facts (*Masson v. New Yorker Magazine*, 1991). The defense can also argue that the communication was privileged. In certain government settings, such as in court or a legislative proceeding, a speaker has an absolute privilege and is immune from any libel suit (Harmon, 2011). The purpose of this immunity is to make sure information flows freely on the floor of legislatures or in court, so informed decisions can be made. But any false statements made in those proceedings may face the harsher criminal penalties of **perjury**.

A person or entity that repeats a defamatory statement can be held liable. But, in many states there is also a qualified immunity for those who republish any defamation communicated in protected government forums, so long as it is an exact repetition of the statement (Harmon, 2011). For example, a journalist could quote a witness in a trial or a legislator on the floor of Congress. But if the journalist was to change the quotes too much or add more content to it, then the journalist may lose the qualified privilege.

Another defense is the distributor's protection. Traditionally, third-party providers of media content, such as wire services, newspaper stands, bookstores, and cable operators could not be sued for libel that it sold to consumers (American Law Institute, 1977, Sec. 581.1). These entities were not considered publishers, because they were not expected to know all the content that they distributed. For digital companies, this defense has been codified in **Sec. 230 of the Communications Decency Act**, which exempts any online third-party providers, so long as they are not the publisher of the information (Communications Decency Act, 1996). Thus, Facebook or Twitter cannot be sued for the information that is posted by its users as they are not expected to be monitoring all the information posted (see Sec. 230 text box).

The most common defense in libel case is opinion and fair comment. Pure opinion is always protected because, by definition, for a statement to rise to the level of defamation it needs to be an assertion of fact. But there is difficulty in defining what is an opinion and what is an assertion of fact.

The U.S. Supreme Court has defined opinion as a statement that cannot be proven true or false (*Milkovich v. Lorain Journal Co.*, 1990). So, calling someone a thief can be proven true or false as they have either stolen or they have not. But calling someone a jerk is an opinion as it cannot be proven true or false—it is purely subjective. Nonetheless, someone may use a word like thief without being literal. As discussed above, context matters. This is sometimes called **rhetorical hyperbole**, which is an exaggeration used to make a point. If a cable news pundit is commenting on how a politician is using taxpayers' money, the person may refer to the politician as being a "thief." But the context suggests that the news pundit is not being literal.

Parody or satire are also protected because they are exaggerations not to be taken seriously. When Alec Baldwin plays Donald Trump on *Saturday Night Live* and portrays him to be colluding with Russia in a treasonous way, this would not be considered libel as the context tells us it is a joke. Moreover, when it comes to criticism, there is more protection, especially when discussing public affairs. When all the elements and defenses are combined, it makes it nearly impossible for a public figure to win a libel case (Shoenberger, 2010).

Two lesser used common law defenses are consent and reight of reply. Consent would be proof that the plaintiff allowed for the defamation to be published. This could be an explicit consent. An example would be when a production studio buys the rights to someone's story. But consent can also be implied, such as commentary on the statement after publication in which the plaintiff says it is acceptable (American Law Institute, 1977, Sec. 583).

The right of reply defense can best be described as an "eye for an eye." This is when the defendant's libelous statement is countered by the plaintiff's libelous response. In a jurisdiction that recognizes this defense, the two are seen to cancel each other out (File, 2017).

Sec. 230: Immunity From Responsibility?

During the infancy of the internet, Congress passed a law meant to protect nascent online companies from the threat of expensive litigation. Sec. 230 of the Communications Decency Act frees third-party digital sites from the liability for their users' post. If someone defames you online, your only recourse is to find the speaker to bring to court—you cannot sue the company that hosts the site or provides the service.

But a generation later, this law has recently come under great scrutiny as online sites have grown in power and impact. Today, the idea that Google or Facebook need special protection from lawsuits for fear of going out of business seems ridiculous. Many critics believe that Sec. 230 now allows for hate speech and defamation to run rampant online and because of the legal shield, social media companies have no reason to try and stop it. Thus, there have been political calls to repeal or amend Sec. 230.

In 2017, Congress passed the Stop Enabling Sex Traffickers Act (SESTA) and the Fight Online Sex Trafficking Act (FOSTA). The legislation was in response to sex traffickers using the online site Backpage.com. The site had been sued by victims of sex trafficking, but the plaintiffs were unable to prevail due to Sec. 230 immunity. But SESTA and FOSTA allow sites to be sued if they knowingly facilitate such criminal activity. Politicians from both sides of the aisle have called for further amending Sec. 230 to regulate social media companies. Democrats have blamed sites for the proliferation of fake news while Republicans have criticized sites for having a liberal bias.

If Sec. 230 were to be repealed, then third-party sites like Google and Facebook could be held liable for what users post, just as they can be held liable for copyright infringement today. These companies would then need to monitor their sites and pull down possibly damaging posts. But would we want tech companies deciding what is defamatory and what is not?

See: Sullivan, M. (2018, November 29). The 1996 law that made the web is in the crosshairs. Fast Company. https://www.fastcompany.com/90273352/maybe-its-time-to-take-awaythe-outdated-loophole-that-big-tech-exploits"

Other Types of False Speech

Historically, false speech has received greater scrutiny from courts. But the U.S. Supreme Court has never held that false speech is categorically unprotected. In some cases, the Court has protected false speech, for example, negligent spreading of falsehoods in the public sphere (*New York Times v. Sullivan*, 1964).

The Court has stated that for false speech to be punished, the speaker would have to have gained something from the false speech (*United States v. Alvarez*, 2012). Examples of false speech that are not protected because they cause a clear harm include defamation, fraud, perjury, obstruction of justice, and false advertising (see Chapter 9). But even with these categories, there is still a requirement that the speaker knew they were speaking falsehoods with an intent to mislead, and there was a material gain (*United States v. Alvarez*, 2012). For example, it is not perjury unless the witness knows they are lying. In advertising, **puffery**, or exaggeration, allows an auto company to make claims that its cars are the best in the world. Although it may not be true, there is no harm in the advertisement.

The scrutiny of false speech lessens when the speech is political in nature. In U.S. jurisprudence, political speech receives the most protection. Political speech is often a debate of ideology and opinion. Because opinions are not statements of facts, they cannot be considered true or false. Also, when it comes to lies in politics, it is difficult to figure out the harm caused. An individual candidate could sue for libel, but it would be difficult to prevail as a public figure. When it comes to harms to the overall political system, there is no one plaintiff that can claim injury (Healy, 2018).

For example, during the 2016 U.S. presidential campaign, fact-checkers found that Donald Trump spread many lies that moved beyond political opinion (Politifact, n.d.). Some supporters of Hillary Clinton claimed these lies were pivotal to her defeat in the campaign (Alterman, 2018). But in an actual lawsuit, it would have been very difficult for Hillary Clinton to show causation. Moreover, it would be too late after the election for a case to have an impact on the outcome.

Some states were concerned about the number of lies in political campaigns and the impact they had on the integrity of the system, so the states passed false campaign speech statutes (Zenor, 2016). The laws varied, but most allowed for a candidate to be punished (fined or forced out of the race), if they knowingly spread lies about other candidates. These laws usually paralleled defamation law by regulating only direct personal attacks and requiring a showing of actual malice.

But courts have routinely overturned these laws, stating that the government could not show any harm to a specific person and that it could not judge what political speech was true or false (*Susan B. Anthony List v. Driehaus*, 2016). Thus, most of these laws are now unenforceable. Opponents of such laws welcomed the judicial decisions arguing that campaign speech laws allowed for the political party who wins to punish the other party. They argued that the answer to false political speech is more truthful political speech (*Susan B. Anthony List v. Driehaus*, 2016).

False Light: A Tort Without a Home

False Light is a tort that protects plaintiffs against published information that has been distorted in a way that injures their reputation. This could include audio or video that has been purposely or negligently edited to make someone look foolish or criminal. Most legal textbooks and statutes put the tort under the umbrella of privacy law as it pertains to truthful information (rather than outright lies). It has also been called *libel light* because it deals with false information that injures a person's reputation.

False light became a popular tort in the late 1960s once the U.S. Supreme Court added a fault standard to libel law, making it very difficult for public figure plaintiffs to win. However, courts quickly caught on that plaintiffs were trying to circumvent libel law. So, the U.S. Supreme Court soon added a fault element to false light cases brought by public figures. Thus, as with libel, it is very difficult to win false light cases and today, the tort is rarely used.

See American Law Institute. (1977). *Restatement of the law, second, torts.* American Law Institute Publishers, Sec. 652(E).
See Time, Inc. V. Hill, 385 U.S. 374 (1967).

Virtual Issues in False Speech and Emerging Media

1. Should the average person's reputation be a matter of public concern?

There are many internet sites and apps that allow people to score their satisfaction with businesses, including individual contractors like doctors, mechanics, plumbers, professors, and so forth. In the past, review sites like Yelp and Angie's List have been at the center of lawsuits by business owners who felt the reviews were defamatory ("Contractor Suing," 2012). But the business owners can only sue the original poster because online sites are immune from defamation cases as they are protected by Sec. 230.

But Yelp is an example of a review site that rates public businesses seeking of customers. Assuming the posts are truthful information, it should be protected speech. Of course, customer reviews are filled with opinion, which is also protected in libel cases. But, when it comes to individuals, should reputations be open to such scrutiny?

As discussed in Chapter 3, China is implementing a social-credit system by tracking people using connected devices and AI. This type of surveillance may seem unsettling, but most Chinese citizens who are aware of the program are in favor of it because they believe it can improve the fabric of the nation (Elgan, 2019). Then there is the app Peeple, which allow users to score people's reputations. It has been described as "Yelp for humans" (Perez, 2016). Originally, the app allowed users to review anyone. But, after public backlash, the developers allowed for people to remove negative reviews or opt-out of being reviewed by paying for the subscription. Of course, they won't see these negative reviews unless they pay (Perez, 2016).

Peeple never took off as an app. Maybe it went too far or maybe the watered-down version was not that different than what people could already do on social media. But it may not be an idea that is dead forever. More democratic nations could adopt a social-credit system like China, through a commercial app (Li, 2018). A "human review" app could use information gathered through all of our connected devices to calculate scores. Social media apps, such as Facebook, Instagram, and Whatsapp, are already connected, and more can be added. Your smart phone can be tracked by Google, so that it knows where you have been and what you have browsed. Amazon can track what you buy and watch. All of this information from your phone can be shared to the other apps you use. The amount of information about your life would quickly add up to enough to make a social judgment about you. These data could be added to outside reviews from people who know you (and, hopefully, like you) as well as assessments from credit companies, consultants, the government, and so forth. The totality would be an individualized reputation score (see Chapter 5 about the privacy issues involved).

A human review app like Peeple would likely claim immunity under Sec. 230. However, this could be questioned as Peeple should be able to foresee that bullying, harassment, and defamation is going to occur. It would be an app built for the sole purpose of building or tearing down reputations. Certainly Peeple would be negligent in allowing this to happen. But social media companies are aware of the amount of harassment that occurs on their platforms, and they have been protected by Sec. 230. You could always sue the person who posts, and if you are not a public figure, they would likely have to prove the information is true. But, much of the commentary could be protected opinion.

Finally, if a social score were to become culturally accepted in the U.S., the argument would be that it is in the **public interest** to improve the fabric of the nation and make people more accountable through public shaming. It is not that absurd to see this happening as public shaming occurs every day on social media (Woodyatt, 2015). If this is the case, maybe our actions and reputations become a matter of public interest. Thus, we all become public figures and would have to prove that scores were calculated based on knowingly false information.

2. Should defamation law protect the reputations of avatars in virtual worlds?

People put a lot of work into their gaming avatars. Sometimes, they are fantastical and magical in nature. But we control the identity of that avatar. Other times, people create avatars that are strikingly similar to themselves. So, if an avatar created by you, looks like you, then do you have reputational rights in the avatar? When other players talk in the games and say defamatory comments about your character, what will be the ability to redress the grievance?

Courts have not yet examined whether an avatar or a new identity in the virtual world has a reputation that can be harmed. To win a libel case, a plaintiff would have to show identification—the audience must know the statement was about you. But it is not clear whether a statement about your avatar identifies you. Celebrities often have alternate personas that differ from their off-stage identities. Yet most of the public comment about them would be about their on stage personas. There is no doubt that celebrities can sue for libel if they can show a harm to their public reputation (Griffe, 2007).

Currently, courts have not recognized a reputational right in avatars absent an injury that moves to the real world. But most of the game developers do have their own rules for users. Hate speech, bullying and others forms of harassment are usually not allowed. If you can report the other gamers, you may be able to have them removed from the forum (Blizzard, 2018). The judgment and punishment then stay within the context of the game.

There could be a situation where the defaming of your avatar permanently hurts your reputation among other players in the forum. For example, they may no longer want to play alongside you as a teammate or now your avatar is attacked every time you play. But whether this rises to defamation is unlikely under current law. The difficulty would be in proving quantifiable harms. It is also unlikely that a jury would be willing to punish a player for such speech—unless of course the jury consisted of players who have also been victims of such character assassination.

An old adage is that we should not believe everything we hear, and this may be especially true online. Much of what is shared is clickbait and lacks in veracity. In some ways, when we go online, we consent to the world of exaggeration and hate that is spewed. Are virtual worlds the same—does exaggeration and hate come with the territory? The gaming community is infamous for its vile verbal attacks, especially against female players. So, does that mean we all assume the risk that our avatars and their reputations are not safe? Moreover, do we want what is said in these virtual worlds to stay in the virtual worlds free from real world consequences?

The fault element of libel law was set up in an era of analog media in which a few corporations controlled the limited channels. It separates between public and private defendants because of the belief that the former had power that allowed them media access and the public goodwill to defend themselves, whereas private citizens did not (DeSimone, 2018). But, in the connected worlds, such a dichotomy may not exist. Today, everyone has access to these channels and can spread a message instantly and infinitely. We may now all be able to defend ourselves equally, thus any defamation must be shown with actual malice. Moreover, does our equal access to the forum then give us an implied right to reply? In other words, if we choose not to defend ourselves in the forum where it occurred, do we relinquish the right to a legal remedy for any harms?

3. Will the explosion of bots spreading disinformation require a reexamination of the right to lie?

As discussed in Chapter 3, the 2016 U.S. presidential election opened the eyes of Americans to an issue that had been affecting other nations for several years. Russia (and other nations) implemented a disinformation campaign to stoke political upheaval in the United States. Russia was not the first nation to do this, and the United States was not the first nation to have been targeted. Though the use of social media was new, the use of disinformation was not. It has been a military tactic dating back to ancient times (Posetti & Matthews, 2018). The U.S. government also used disinformation throughout the 20th century to control foreign nations and change world events, such as events at the Gulf of Tonkin and claims of weapons of mass destruction in Iraq (Posetti & Matthews, 2018).

But the Russian government's use of disinformation in 2016 was unique for two reasons. First, the United States and its advanced security systems seemed previously invulnerable (Mejias & Vokuev, 2018). Second, Russia's use of bots allowed it to overwhelm media systems with constant messaging, thereby, building its own echo chamber allowing it to reinforce the disinformation that it was creating, making it seem more truthful.

Russia's Internet Research Agency (IRA) created fervor by targeting different political coalitions with incendiary political opinion. In some instances, the IRA spread outright lies such as posing as ISIS hackers and threatening military spouses (Hanns Siedel Foundation, 2019). It also promoted misinformation about public health issues by siding with antivaxxers with messages like, "Did you know there was a secret government database of #vaccine-damaged children? #VaccinateUS" (Kirk, 2019, para. 6).

Social media companies like Facebook are now aware of the extent of the issue and have begun to implement their own AI to fight the problem. During the 2018 U.S. midterm election, Facebook was able to remove over 45,000 accounts that spread lies about voting information in an attempt to suppress turnout (Fried, 2019).

The race for better technology between the trolls and the platforms will continue with each one taking temporary leads. But the platforms are at a disadvantage. Even if they wanted to stop disinformation, they would have to be able to decide what is true or false. In attempts by state governments to regulate false speech in political campaigns, courts have deemed the attempts unconstitutional because they left the governments to be "truth commissions," deciding what was right or wrong.

The free speech approach to regulating lies has been to allow more counter-speech that supports the truth (*United States v. Alvarez*, 2012). Ultimately, private platforms do not have to follow the First Amendment; thus, they can decide what is true and what is not. Nonetheless, the concern is still the same: Will these platforms have even more power as a "ministry of truth" without any legal remedies available to those who are deemed to be spreading lies (Palmer, 2018).

Under current false speech laws, lies can be regulated if they cause a harm to another, such as in cases of fraud, perjury, or false advertising. But simply lying is not illegal. If more governments, organizations, or persons develop AI to flood the marketplace with false information, it will be quite difficult to stop them with legal remedies unless the plaintiff can show evidence of gain for the entity that unleashed the bot. Because social media companies make money from having users create data, and Sec. 230 protects them from liability for the actions of third parties, there seems to be little incentive to stop misinformation outside of political pressure. With the amount of information now available, it is arguable that the government may need to start regulating content by looking at the intent of the speaker, not just the consequences.

CASE STUDY
To Tell the Truth?

Lying is inherently human. Plants and animals will instinctively mimic and disguise in order to survive. But to consciously send misleading information in order to distort reality is unique to us, since our reality is a social construct. If enough us believe something to be, then we accept it as a reality. Alternatively, even in the face of overwhelming evidence, some of us refuse to accept some things as reality.

Advanced AI will have to be programmed with a sense of reality. For it, there will be one truth only with everything else being a lie. This may make communication with humans quite difficult. Humans lie a lot. Sometimes we lie to protect others or to save face. Sometimes we lie with a wink through sarcasm, hyperbole, or rhetorical flair. But will AI recognize this gray area of truth and nuance in communication?

Twitter created a bot called Tay that was to learn from chatting with others online. Within 24 hours, it had turned vile, spreading lies including claiming that British comedian "[R]icky [G]ervais learned totalitarianism from [A] dolf [H]itler, the inventor of atheism" (Victor, 2016, para. 5). Microsoft shut down Tay and redeveloped the bot, and to date, there has been no such issue

(Victor, 2016). The nonprofit OpenAI created software called GPT2 that could create complex text including news and fictional stories. The organization claimed it was the most complex text-creating AI developed as it could write long passages without malfunctioning. It also understood syntax and correctly guessed passages in already published work. It was an exciting development, but the group was unwilling to publicly share it just yet, because they had not protected it from being used maliciously to spread what it called "deepfake texts" (Hern, 2019). These two examples are isolated, and their works may be easy to spot. But, as we have seen with online disinformation campaigns, bots can easily dominate the marketplace of ideas. They can be produced by the thousands and be constantly chatting. Thus, they can change the reality and what is truth.

AI will be given a reality when its programmed. But when it comes to politics and morality—two very subjective areas—someone will have to program the truth in to AI. Finding one truth will be difficult. Finally, if AI advances to be more human-like, it could have its own multiple interpretations of realities. If it evolves further, passing human intellect to the point of creating its own intelligence, then one day, it may be programming our reality.

Discussion Questions

1. Will advanced AI be able to lie or will it be too logical? Why or why not?

2. Should advanced AI be able to lie in some circumstances? How should it be programmed to do so?

3. Should there be regulation that prohibits AI's ability to lie? What should be the rules?

4. Should advanced AI be used to judge if humans are lying? Why or why not?

CHAPTER 5

Privacy and Security

The Chinese government has been applying facial recognition technology throughout the country to surveil its citizens. In one instance, Chinese law enforcement used the technology to spot a suspect in a concert crowd of 50,000 people (O'Dowd, 2018). This would seem to be a good thing as a suspect was caught, but what if the technology is being used to find people who are not criminals at all? Rather, they are just critics of the government.

China may be the most aggressive nation in its adoption of the technology, but it is not the only place where citizens are being tracked. In the United States, Facebook uses facial recognition AI to identify users. Google sells a doorbell that identifies people who pass by your door and then sends a text to you. Apple's iPhone can be opened with a smile (Gebhart, 2019).

This technology is also being used by the U.S. government for **surveillance**, or constant monitoring of people and places. For example, Amazon has been marketing its facial recognition technology to law enforcement agencies across the country. This technology allows police to identify a person's face, even if it is mostly blocked (Wingfield, 2018). Of course, federal and state law enforcement have been using facial recognition technology for years to track suspects. But its implementation has not been equally distributed as police have focused such efforts in low-income neighborhoods—sometimes even before any crime has been committed (Gurchiek, 2012).

Generally, people do not have an expectation of privacy in public. We are used to being constantly photographed by cell phones, private security cameras, and traffic light cameras. But now, facial recognition technology allows these pictures to be analyzed using photos from mug shots to driver's licenses to social media posts. Security cameras have been around for decades, and investigators review these videos to find someone who had done something suspicious. But now, facial recognition technology combined with AI processing will enable massive amounts of data to be analyzed in real time. This constant surveillance will become commonplace. Since privacy law is rooted in our social expectation—if we can always expect to be monitored-then we will no longer have an expectation of privacy.

This chapter examines how advancement in technology may influence our expectation of privacy. First, it discusses contemporary law for privacy, surveillance, and data security. Second, it investigates the looming issues with emerging technology that could affect our expectation of privacy.

Legal Principles in Privacy

Privacy law is usually divided into four sub-areas: 1) Intrusion upon Seclusion; 2) Publication of Private Facts; 3) False Light; and 4) Right to Publicity (Keeton & Prosser, 1984). The first two sub-torts mirror popular conceptions of privacy and will be discussed in this chapter. The other two sub-torts are closer to other areas of the laws. False Light is more akin to Defamation (Chapter 4), and Right to Publicity is more akin to Intellectual Property Law (Chapter 7), so are discussed in those chapters.

History of Privacy Law

Privacy law is a relatively recent concept. Its growth parallels the development of mass media. In U.S. jurisprudence, scholars often cite its genesis to be 1890 with the publication of an article by Samuel Warren and Louis Brandies in the *Harvard Law Review*. Privacy law was then codified over the early part of the 20th century, and by mid-century it was entrenched in U.S. law.

Currently, we live in an era of conflicted privacy rights. We have more privacy laws than ever before. Yet, at the same time, as a society, we collect and share more information than ever before. Moreover, with the advancement of technology, information seems less safe than it has ever been. We are constantly under surveillance from the government and corporations. People who are looking to steal information and use it for personal gain have tools at their disposal that make it quite simple. The profit from stealing far outweighs the chances of being caught (Stewart, 2015).

Expectation of Privacy and Intrusion

Generally, Intrusion is the illegal collection of information. This can be either criminal or civil in nature. In many ways, intrusion is similar to physical trespass of property. If a person passes a certain boundary, then they may be liable. With intrusion, it is the act that is judged, not the information collected.

The general rule for **intrusion** is whether the plaintiff had a "reasonable expectation of privacy." This is both subjective and objective. The subjective aspect belongs to the plaintiff and if there was a personal expectation of privacy. The objective aspect is the cultural acceptance of what is reasonable privacy. Over time this reasonableness can change, often because of the expansion of technology. A few decades ago, the idea of publicly discussing sexuality or health concerns would have been taboo. Now, we often do this on social media without much trepidation.

Generally, there is no expectation of privacy in public places. If someone overhears you talking at a park, you do not have a privacy claim because you are in a public setting and assume a risk that someone will overhear you. This is true in any space open to the public, including privately owned businesses.

But there are some exceptions to the general rule—we do have limited times when we are in public but expect privacy. For example, when you use a credit card machine at a grocery store or restaurant, you cover up the keypad, so no one can see your PIN. If someone were following you and trying to take it, you may have a privacy claim (and a criminal charge as well) (*Nader v. General Motors Corporation*, 1970). Another example of privacy in public places is that people always maintain a small distance of personal space. The U.S. Supreme Court has held that people entering abortion clinics have a small privacy bubble, and protesters cannot invade it or stop people from entering the premises (*Hill v. Colorado*, 2000; *McCullen v. Coakley*, 2014).

When it comes to private property the rules are not as clear. Stores and restaurants are private property, but they are open to the public. So, if someone overhears you at a restaurant, it would be difficult to claim privacy. If you were sitting in a waiting room at the doctor's office and people see you and tell others, it would be difficult to claim privacy. People saw you in plain sight and were allowed to be there. However, the back offices of a store may be considered private, and certainly what you and your doctor discuss in the exam room is private. Of course, the patient is free to share the information— the doctor/patient **confidentiality** belongs to the patient, not the doctor.

A person has the greatest expectation of privacy in the home. But it is not absolute. If you are standing in your driveway, yard, or even in front of a window, your actions may not be private. If a passer-by on a public sidewalk sees you, then there is no expectation of privacy. If a neighbor can see you from their property, then there is no expectation of privacy. However, this assumes they are using unassisted sight and hearing. If the neighbor is using a technological enhancement, the answer may be different (*Kyllo v. United States*, 2001).

When it comes to technological enhancement, the question is whether there is an objective expectation of privacy. If the neighbor is using a telescope or binoculars, there may not be a claim as these instruments are readily available and we would expect that people have them. But if the technology is so new or so advanced that we would not expect the average person to be using it, then we would have an expectation of privacy (*United States v. Jones*, 2012). A generation ago, if someone had a drone and flew it over our house, that would have been unexpected and seemed like an invasion of privacy. Today, it may not, as long as the drone stays high enough and does not trespass onto our property (*California v. Ciraolo*, 1986).

It is often believed that lying to gain access to a property is illegal, but this is usually not the case. The act of lying is not illegal per se; instead, one must look at what the lie garnered. If the lie gets the defendant access that they would not have gained but for the lie, then it is considered **false pretenses** and is illegal. For example, if a journalist walks into a supermarket open to the public in order to film an exposé about the working conditions, this will not be considered false pretenses, even if the journalist lies about why she is there. The supermarket is open to the public, and the store owners assume the risk that what people see will be reported. But suppose the reporter creates a fake resume—withholding information about being a reporter—to gain employment at the supermarket. As an employee, she has access to parts of the store and conversations not open to the public. This would be false pretenses because the lie gets her special access (*Food Lion v. Capital Cities/ABC*, 1999).

Government Surveillance

The right to privacy derives from the Fourth Amendment, which dictates how law enforcement can gather information in a criminal investigation (Zimmerman, 2012). If a person is the target of a criminal investigation, the police must respect his or her reasonable expectation of privacy (the same rule for civil intrusion law). If the defendant has a reasonable expectation of privacy, then generally, the police will need to get a warrant in order to search the person or place (*Griffin v. Wisconsin*, 1987).

As with civil privacy law, criminal defendants have the most protection in their homes (*Chimel v. California*, 1969). Police can rarely enter a home without the person's consent or a judge-issued warrant. But, to get a warrant, an officer needs to show **probable cause**, or a good reason, for search or arrest.

If the police is able to show probable cause after the arrest, then they may proceed without a warrant (*Terry v. Ohio*, 1968). For example, if an officer walks by a house and hears gunshots and screaming or sees a drug sale in the driveway, then the officer can approach the scene. This is acceptable because the officer can clearly hear the gunshot or clearly see the transaction, so it is probable that a crime is taking place (*Terry v. Ohio*, 1968). But if an officer uses a recording device placed in the home to record conversations about criminal behavior, then it would not be admissible in court without a prior warrant (*Katz v. United States*, 1967). Ultimately, as with privacy law, if suspects are in public or can be detected without special enhancements, then they likely do not have a Fourth Amendment defense when they are arrested.

The internet is public, so generally activity online is not private. Even if you are using your phone at home behind closed doors, once you connect to the internet, you are in a public forum. It is parallel to being in a public park. Thus, whatever you do is open to surveillance if the site is open to the public, and your account is not set to private. Police can monitor social media sites and web traffic that are public. Any evidence that is collected can be used against a plaintiff (Crowther, 2012). However, the site must be open to a public search. Other information gathered by companies, such as cell phone locations and emails, cannot be ascertained by the police without a warrant or consent.

After 9/11, U.S. citizens feared for their safety. Often, in times of fear, people are willing to give up some of their civil liberties for a feeling of more safety. Thus, shortly after the attacks Congress passed the U.S. Patriot Act (2001), which gave the government sweeping powers in its fight against terrorism. Critics argued that it greatly eroded the Fourth Amendment and privacy protections for the nation (Rosenzweig, 2004). The Act allowed surveillance of anyone suspected of being a terrorist, but also anyone who was thought to be associated with them. Moreover, law enforcement could spy on U.S. citizens, who were suspected to have connections with terrorists, without triggering constitutional protections, such as a need to show probable cause. Much of this government surveillance was not known to the public. Most searches were approved by **Federal Intelligence Surveillance Court (FISC)**, the court charged with approving surveillance pertaining to national security risks from foreign agents in the United. States. The FISC's decisions are neither made public nor is there any oversight by other branches of government (United States Foreign Intelligence Surveillance Court, n.d.).

In 2007, Congress passed the Protect America Act, which allowed the NSA to collect mass data from phone and internet companies under the auspices of the FISC. The act was meant to allow the government to investigate foreign intelligence targets outside the United States. The third-party phone and internet companies could not tell targets that the government had requested their records. It also expanded the government's ability to wiretap suspects and collect information (Protect America Act, 2007).

The NSA's surveillance programs became a controversial issue when whistle-blower Edward Snowden revealed the extent of the information gathering. The Protect America Act allowed the government to track which sites were visited and for how long. It also enabled the government to collect information about emails headers, Google searches, social media activity, and so forth (Ackerman, 2016). Most concerning, the surveillance sweeps collected information from U.S. citizens who were not intelligence targets.

In 2015, Congress passed the USA Freedom Act, which extended the U.S. Patriot Act but no longer allowed NSA to use unauthorized mass surveillance. The act now required the NSA to send individual inquiries to the phone and internet companies in order to access information. Critics argue that the new act still allows too much protected information to be collected, and that with changing communication technology such as encryption and VPNs, mass surveillance is no longer effective (Landau, 2019). At the end of 2019, Congress is considering reauthorization of the act.

Private Surveillance

The Fourth Amendment places a high bar on government attempts to surveil citizens. But private actors are not bound by the Fourth Amendment (*Burdeau v. McDowell*, 1921). Thus, private persons and corporations can collect information with fewer restrictions. For example, every online site you visit sends back **cookies** that leave a marker on your device (until erased). Sites can also collect information about the devices you used, or **digital fingerprinting**, which can be used to track activities on your apps.

Everything we post online is permanent and rarely ever erased. The data are processed, shared widely and, most often, sold for profit. Many consumers enjoy the permanence because, with this access, each site can serve them better by saving passwords, offering suggestions, using analytics, and so forth. However, others argue that it is a gross violation of our privacy rights as most of it happens without details being revealed to us (Jerome, 2013).

In the United States, there is currently very little consumer protection against the collection and dissemination of this information. Consumers can attempt to protect themselves by using private browsers, VPNs, and sites that promise confidentiality. But even those offer only limited protection (Noyes, 2015).

Despite several federal attempts to regulate online privacy, the only current U.S. regulation pertains to online activity regarding children under the age of 13 who are not allowed to give out personal information without consent from a parent (Children's Online Privacy Protection Act, 1998). However, in the European Union, there is much greater privacy protection online. In 2016, the EU passed General Data Protection Regulations, which require sites to use strict privacy protections, to disclose all tracking, and to gain consent from consumers. The impact of the law has extended beyond the EU. California passed a similar law in 2018. Since that time most U.S. users have seen a disclosure on sites reporting that they use cookies to track users (Balke, 2018).

The EU also recognizes the **right to be forgotten**, which means that some public information cannot be stored and made available forever. Thus, search engines such as Google must scrub certain information like older criminal records (Ready, 2019). Although the United States has discussed greater privacy protections, there has not been much movement toward a right to be forgotten. Ultimately, it would be very difficult for a right to be forgotten to be recognized in the United States because it would likely violate the First Amendment (Larson III, 2013).

Bringing the Fourth Amendment Into the 21st Century

The law takes a while to catch up to changes in technology. This is especially true with the U.S. Supreme Court, which must wait for cases to filter through the circuit courts before they reach it. Though the Court is often hesitant when it comes to analyzing technology, three recent cases show that justices may be considering the drastic changes occurring in U.S. society. In 2012, the U.S. Supreme Court held that police needed a warrant in order to place a GPS tracker on a suspect's car. In 2014, the Court held that police needed a warrant to search a person's cell phone. In 2018, the Court held that police needed a warrant in order to get a suspect's cell tower position from a telecomm company. These three cases show that the Court recognizes that as we give away more information, we need to have our protection from search and seizure protected. As Justice Sotomayor argued, "Whatever the societal expectations, they can attain constitutionally protected status only if our Fourth Amendment jurisprudence ceases to treat secrecy as a prerequisite for privacy."

See *United States v. Jones*, 565 U.S. 400 (2012)
See *Riley v. California*, 573 U.S. 373 (2014)
See *Carpenter v. United States*, 585 U.S. ___ (2018)

Protecting Information

Today, information is under a constant threat of being gathered and misused. Stolen identities, credit card numbers, social security numbers, and so forth, can be collected and traded very easily through digital media (Somani, 2018). Authorities are constantly trying to keep up with the deluge of stolen information being used. It may seem as though our information is less protected than ever, but when it comes to statutory protections, there are more laws protecting privacy than ever before.

In the United States, there are several major statutes that often play a role in everyday situations. For example, the Health Insurance Portability Privacy and Accountability Act (HIPAA) of 1996 protects health records from being disclosed without a patient's consent. Critics have argued that it is overused and cited when it is not applicable. Journalists argue that polices officers will often cite HIPAA when it comes to blocking information about crimes and accidents, but that HIPAA does not actually apply in those instances (Boni-Saenz, 2007). Another example is the Federal Educational Rights and Privacy Act of 1974 (FERPA), which protects educational records. School administrators, teachers, and other employees are not allowed to give out records, such as grades, without consent. For those under 18 years old, the right of consent belongs to parents. But for college students, the right belongs to them, and schools cannot give education records to anyone without the student's consent (U.S. Department of Education, 2007).

The statutes above are examples of specific information that is protected. Most states also protect information generally through the *publication of private fact* tort (American Law Institute, 1977, Sec. 652d). A person can sue when someone publishes previously undisclosed information that would be offensive to publish. This tort requires publicity—or a mass publishing—not just telling another person. Today, this would include publishing on a social media site where hundreds of people could see it instantly. The information also has to be previously undisclosed. If the plaintiff has told several people already, he or she could not then attempt to sue one particular person for divulging the information. Finally, the publication of the information needs to be offensive. With the amount of personal information that we divulge about ourselves on social media, it is difficult to consider any information would be offensive to publish. We freely talk about sexuality, diseases, and other situation that were once considered taboo (Taylor, 2005).

Finally, even private information we want to protect can be published if it is newsworthy. Throughout the last 50 years it has seemed like less and less is considered too scandalous to publish, and everything is of interest to the public. But, in a significant case, pro wrestler Hulk Hogan sued Gawker for publishing a video of him having sex with his friend's wife. Hogan's friend had consented to the act and recorded it (*Gawker Media, LLC v. Bollea*, 2015). Gawker argued that it was newsworthy because Hogan was a celebrity, and it was not a secret as he had bragged about it on the radio. But Hogan argued that he had two personas: the celebrity personality of Hulk Hogan and the private personality of Terry Bollea (his real name). A jury in Florida agreed with Hogan and awarded him $140 million. The award threatened to put Gawker out of business, so it appealed the case. In the interim, the company was bought out, and the new parent company settled for $31 million (and all Gawker properties were placed under Gizmodo Media Group). Although we will not know the outcome of the case, it indicates that the protection of privacy, even for celebrities, may be returning.

Virtual Issues in Privacy/Security in Emerging Media

1. **Should information shared through connected devices, such as phones, cars, and appliances, be considered protected as private information free from access by corporations and government?**

Every few months it seems the headlines reveal a massive data breach. In 2014, hackers accessed 3 billion Yahoo accounts that included information on names, dates of birth, email addresses, and passwords. In 2018, Marriott announced that hackers had stolen information from 500 million accounts, many of which included credit card numbers and dates. Equifax revealed that hackers had accessed 143 million accounts and took information on social security numbers and driver's licenses (Armerding, 2018).

Of the legal issues surrounding emerging technology, the concern of data collection has received the most popular press coverage. People have been concerned with the amount of data collected by governments and corporations alike. With the billions of connected devices collecting information 24/7, it brings significant questions about privacy in the 21st century.

Generally, the law centers on our expectation of privacy. This is fact specific to the person and situation, but it is also a cultural determination. In the digital era, our collective expectation of privacy is evolving. As new technology becomes more commonplace, our expectation of privacy decreases (Goodwin, 2018). The idea that our phone will listen and understand us was once absurd, but now this is well accepted. Most connected devices can listen to us, even when we are not talking to them directly. All this information can be collected and stored, and, for the most part, we are powerless over it. Today, privacy advocates are concerned with the access that digital assistants such as Amazon's Alexa and Google Assistant, and their parent companies, are given. These two companies have a business model built on the collecting, using, and selling of data (Lynskey, 2019). But they have become another technology to which we consent; thus, we find it difficult to argue for our privacy when it shares information.

With our phone apps we sign terms and conditions that inform us that they are collecting information. Although many of us do not read terms of services, we are mostly aware that they are collecting information (Berreby, 2017). As consumers, we welcome the surveillance because it can be used to provide better service. We may enjoy directed ads that show us products we are interested in or talk-to-text as it is easier and quicker, and we do not have to worry about spelling (although we do have to worry about enunciation). **Geotagging** allows us to share where a photo was taken or have reminders about places we want to visit.

In exchange for these services, we often ignore or are unaware of the other uses for the information, such as consumer research, advertising to others, and the sale of our data to other companies. Even though the terms of service are mostly transparent, and we agree to it, we do not get to negotiate the terms. We may feel comfortable in giving information to the companies that support our devices and apps, but it does not mean we want it shared with the world.

Information databases, cloud storage, and connected devices can also be used by law enforcement for gathering intelligence (Simpson, 2017). We have the highest expectation of privacy in our home, and generally police need a warrant to enter it. But people who are using AI-powered virtual assistants in their homes have a device that collects a lot of information. The devices certainly share the information with the companies that run them. But can law enforcement access them? The answer depends on the definition of public.

When we share information on social media, even if we are in our homes, we have made it public. Thus, law enforcement can monitor and use information from these public platforms (Taylor, 2014). However, we do have privacy interests in our phones; police cannot just take them and open them without a warrant. So, with AI assistants it would depend where the information is stored. Police would probably need a warrant to take the actual device, but may have an easier time accessing the stored information (McLaughlin, 2017). In the past, companies were much more willing to share information with authorities, especially if it was remotely linked to national security ("Cooperation," 2018). However, over the last decade, as public perception has changed, companies have been more reluctant to work with law enforcement without a warrant (Apuzzo et al., 2015).

Federal and state statutes protect much of the information shared with third parties online. For example, the Video Privacy Protection Act, passed in 1988 and updated in 2012, protects information shared with video services, so Netflix cannot tell others what we are watching without our consent. Government could pass specific laws protecting the information shared on connected devices. Such laws would make it more difficult for companies to conduct business and sell the data in the United States, but it would protect privacy (Kang, 2014). However, no law would keep the information completely safe from hackers.

2. **Should there be privacy and anonymity for our identities in a virtual world? Should there be a right to be forgotten in the real-world identity?**

Surveillance in virtual worlds is not a legal issue. As with social media, anyone who has access to the medium can use it to collect information. Any privacy protections are offered by the creator of the virtual world. Thus, there is no privacy in what you or your avatar do in these worlds. For example, the police can join a game and surveil the actions of the avatar, and this would not be a violation of expectation of privacy. Anyone could report what you did in these virtual worlds as the information would not be considered to be private facts (Pridmore & Overocker, 2014).

Moreover, similar to social media, it is difficult to believe that we as a society would find it offensive to discuss what occurs in these open virtual forums. However, if the company that created the platform stated that it was to be a private forum, then there would be an expectation among those who used the platform that it would remain so. There could be an argument in privacy or contract law.

But, as we spend more time in virtual worlds, we may begin to develop an expectation of privacy within them. In the real world there is a general private/public property dichotomy. But even in some public places we can have an expectation of privacy. If virtual worlds mimic the real world, then the same should hold true. If in virtual worlds we have something akin to a house where our avatars retreat to and do not allow most other avatars to enter, then this could be considered an expectation of privacy in this virtual space. Of course, since the world was created by a developer who may always have access to all spaces in the virtual world, then any expectation of privacy may be defeated. Once again, the terms of service will dictate the privacy rights in these worlds.

Immersing ourselves in virtual worlds is often an escape from reality. We take on different personas and often move in anonymity. Under U.S. law, we have a right to anonymity; speakers do not have to disclose their identity. In the EU, there is also right to be forgotten and not have all information about yourself be readily available to the public. But in a digital world of surveillance, this is more and more difficult to obtain. One solution is a development of a virtual world where we all start with new identities, and privacy is protected. Of course, the developers of this software would have to guarantee such protections and decide not to make a profit off trading collected data.

3. Should AI in our homes be designed to protect our privacy, or should it have to report our private actions if it suspects wrongdoing?

AI will learn through processing massive amounts of information. By definition, privacy concerns information that we do not want collected. Currently, our world is inundated with devices collecting information from smart phones to cameras on street corners to reward cards where we shop. Any information that is put into a database is being processed to find trends, patterns, and correlations.

When we use apps, internet sites, rewards card, etc. there is an agreement in the terms of service that the company will collect information from us for processing. Moreover, this information is often given to third parties—which we agree to. We receive marketing online and in the mail because of the information that is collected.

For the most part, companies do not care about the individual. They want the **big data** sets in order to access patterns to turn around and market back to the consumers (Hill, 2012). Oftentimes, what is sold back to you is based on previous activity, but sometimes it is a prediction based on what other people like you are already doing. And, oftentimes they are right (Hill, 2012). As machine learning becomes more precise, AI may be able to reconstruct you with just a handful of facts about you. The predictability of the AI may, in turn, establish your identity, making you into a **self-fulfilling prophecy**. In other words, the AI may one day know you better than you know yourself.

AI assistants like Alexa and Siri are common in households. Today, the voices are usually coming from a small speaker. But soon, they may be replaced by automatons. Our relationship with them may become more like the ones we have with household pets. We will talk with them and share information, even secrets, which may lead to a relationship that is more human-like in nature. Thus, we will have to trust them with our secrets, and by design, manufacturers will want to make them trustworthy and protect confidentiality. But, if robots are designed to be logical, it may not be inherent for them to keep secrets (Everett et al., 2017). If they learn by mimicking human behaviors, then they may also start to keep their own secrets. But, is keeping secrets fundamental to becoming more human?

For example, if an AI is in the home and monitoring a person, it will certainly be able to report what is happening. An AI assistant could be programmed to call the police if it witnesses domestic violence. There will be a question of whether it can be used as evidence in any such crime. The AI may be like a cell phone, and a subpoena could be used to access information, or it could be considered a closer confidant and may one day be protected by *confidentiality law* like spouses, clergy, psychiatrists, and so forth. There could also be a situation in which the AI assistant is analyzing a person's cues. The AI could sense that the person is exhibiting signs of alcoholism, depression, or violence. AI could be designed to detect such behaviors and report them to authorities, even if the person does not want it to do so.

Of course, robots can be programmed to learn privacy, but privacy is fundamentally subjective. It is an individual expectation that shifts with cultural changes. It will be difficult to teach a robot to understand when something is private because people have had difficulty with the social definitions, and courts have had difficulty with legal definitions.

Finally, if a robot fails to protect a person's privacy, there is the question of who can be sued—the manufacturer, the owner of the robot, or the robot itself. The question may be moot, because once privacy is invaded, it is difficult to get back.

CASE STUDY
Sleeping on the Job?

The healthcare industry is one of the biggest parts of the U.S. economy (Lagasse, 2018). When we include the medical profession, insurance, as well as the exercise and nutrition industry it makes up 18% of the U.S. GDP (Sawyer & Cox, 2018).

As with other industries, technology has changed healthcare. These days, we have at our disposal connected devices that collect a vast amount of health information including heart rate, sleep patterns, blood sugar, movement, and so forth. This information can be given to doctors to aid in the diagnosis of health conditions. We also use personal apps that collect and store this information. These apps can use AI to process the information to give us individualized plans for health and fitness (Marshall, 2018).

However, this personal health information can also be shared with other companies, including those that work in the healthcare industry. For example, Google's Project Nightingale houses millions of patients' records for a large health care company, Ascension. Google already owns the personal fitness tracker Fitbit in addition to all the other information it has on users. Google claims that it is abiding by federal law and not using the health information for marketing purposes on its other platforms (Bond, 2019).

Having a central data-system for health information is important when it is health care professionals to whom we want to give the information. But it can also be accessed by health insurance companies to assess consumers and the kind of coverage they will provide (Bond, 2019). Rates may be determined by the overall health of those who are on the plan, though under current U.S. law, pre-existing conditions cannot be considered for denial or prices of plans. If a doctor decides that a patient needs a heart bypass, but the information collected from the person's devices show a decade of poor nutrition and fitness, should that be grounds for denial?

Moreover, 56% of Americans receive their health insurance from their employers. Health care coverage is one the most expensive costs for employers. Over the last decade, many employers have moved toward promoting wellness programs as a way to lower insurance costs, including offering gym memberships and other perks. Recently, there has been a shift to providing connected devices such as Fitbits to promote employee wellness (Landi, 2016).

Today, employers can check employee email accounts because they provide the service and are the owners of the accounts. This same reasoning could extend to fitness devices provided by employers. When people use company property, such as email, cars, smart phones, and so forth, they can be fired for using the property in a way that employers do not approve. But will this extend to information collected from health devices? With the cost of health insurance, there will be an incentive for employers to collect such information and to make bottom line decisions based upon it.

Discussion Questions

1. Should it be illegal for employers to have access to information from connected devices, even if they provide the device? Why or why not?

2. Should health information be used to determine terms of employment? What about insurance benefits? If so, how?

3. If the devices record information about habits such as drug use, should that be used to dismiss an employee? Why or why not?

4. What if sleep patterns reveal the employee is a public danger and legal liability, should an employer be able to act? If so, to what extent?

CHAPTER 6

Civil Liability

I n 2015, Mattel put out Hello Barbie, the first speaking version of the famous doll. The company teamed with ToyTalk, Inc., to enable the doll to interact with children. But in order for it to respond, the toy had to record conversations, and the information was then stored in the cloud (Komando, 2015). It seemed like an advanced toy that would bring happiness to a child, but a group of parents disagreed.

Lawyers for the parents brought a class action lawsuit against Mattel and two other companies involved in creating the toy. The lawsuit argued that a hacker could trick a child by impersonating the doll and lure the child to give information like names, schools, and addresses. The parents sued the company for negligence and invasion of privacy, claiming that their children suffered "emotional distress" (Kearn, 2015).

Of course, if hackers ever did take control of the doll, they would be committing several crimes. But this lawsuit was against the manufacturer for **civil liability**. The argument was that the manufacturer created a product that presented an undue risk. The case was dismissed because no incident had occurred; thus, there was no injury. But, was the case so frivolous? Was the claim of a possible injury so far-fetched?

Companies that put products into the stream of commerce have a duty to make sure they are safe for use. For decades, plaintiffs have attempted to sue media producers, ranging from radio to film to video games, on a theory of negligence. The argument has been that the use of the product was dangerous because it caused someone to commit violence. In most cases, the media companies have won because they are purely entertainment content with expressive value. However, with emerging media, the line may not be so clear as entertainment content becomes more immersive.

This chapter examines how advancement in communication technology can affect product liability for media and tech companies. First, it discusses legal principles of civil liability in negligence, incitement, emotional distress, and harassment. Second, it presents issues of civil liability for emerging media products.

Legal Principles of Civil Liability

Strict Liability and Negligence

Any company that places a product into the stream of commerce owes a **duty of care** to its customers that it will be reasonably safe (American Law Institute, 2010). But, from time-to-time, products will cause injury. Thus, consumers need to have a legal recourse. State law differs but most include three claims for recovery: strict liability, common law negligence, and breach of warranty (Owen & Davis, 2014).

For "goods" that have a design flaw that causes an injury, then there is **strict liability** for the company that produced it (American Law Institute, 2010, Sec. A1b.). As long as the product reached the customer in the condition in which it was shipped, the company will assume the costs if the product causes any injury (Senagore, 2010). If an injury occurs in the application of the product or services, then **products liability** law may allow consumers to sue under the tort of **negligence** (American Law Institute, 2010). Negligence is more difficult to prove than a strict liability case, because it moves beyond just the injury occurring. In a negligence case the plaintiff has to prove four elements: 1) an injury to the plaintiff; 2) a duty of care on part of the defendant; 3) the injury to the plaintiff was foreseeable to the defendant; and 4) the defendant's product was the proximate cause of the injury (Prosser, 1964, p. 148).

Injury is the easiest of the elements to prove. What is more difficult to prove is that the product caused the injury, and its producers should have foreseen it. **Proximate cause** and **foreseeability** are questions of fact for the jury. If a person is driving a riding lawn mower and the blade cuts his or her foot, then it is a direct cause. But suppose the blade gets loose and flies across the yard, hitting a tree. The tree crashes onto a passing car and injures the passenger. It will be much more difficult to prove that the manufacturer could have foreseen such an injury and that the riding lawn mower would be the cause of the injury. Nonetheless, foreseeability is the most important elements for plaintiffs to prove as it is often seen as creating a duty and proving causation (Perry, 2003).

A defendant can win the case if there is **contributory negligence** on the part of the plaintiff. Courts will examine how the consumer used the product. For example, products come with instructions, which often include **waivers of liability**. If a consumer does not use the product as designed, then that may eliminate any liability. Courts usually apply a "reasonable person" criteria to analyze the elements of products liability (Votruba, 2013).

If a third person uses the product and that person's use of the product causes an injury, producers can still be held liable under the theory of **vicarious liability**. This is most often seen in cases in which an employer is sued for its employees' actions. However, for manufacturers of products, these cases are rare as the separate act by the third person usually breaks the chain of causation. Nonetheless, courts may still recognize vicarious liability if the product gave an opportunity for the conduct that was foreseeable (Prosser, 1964). For example, if a bar continues to serve someone who is visibly intoxicated, it is foreseeable that the person could get into a car and cause a fatality.

For media products, negligence is more difficult for the plaintiff to prove than it is with other consumer products (Dee, 2000). Most media products are a form of speech; thus they are protected by the First Amendment, so have a lesser duty of care to their customers (*Davidson v. Time Warner, Inc*, 1997). Foreseeability is easier to prove in media negligence cases. By definition, this element examines whether the event should have been reasonably expected. In these media negligence cases, a plaintiff often sues because someone imitated the content. Since there have long been claims that people are inspired by entertainment to commit violence, it is now foreseeable that others will mimic media content. But, ultimately, proximate cause is the most difficult element to prove as it relies on social science research, which suggests that media effects are not direct or strong (see *Brown v. Entertainment Merchants Association*, 2011). Although an obsession with violent media may give people final inspiration, there are too many other variables that lead to the action both before and after they have watched a movie or played a video game (*James v. Meow Media*, 2002).

There have been several cases of entertainment producers being sued including the board game *Dungeons and Dragons* (*Watters v. TSR, Inc.*, 1990), the movie *Basketball Dairies* (*James v. Meow Media*, 2002), and recording artist Tupac Shakur (*Davidson v. Time Warner*, 1997). In each case, the courts held that there were too many intervening variables in the causation of the injury, mainly the third party who committed the crimes. More recently, Snapchat was sued for negligence in two cases in which teenage drivers caused an accident when trying to get the Snapchat speedometer filter over 100 mph (Lancaster, 2020). In these cases, the courts have been split as to whether Snapchat was protected by Sec. 230 of the CDA.

Incitement Tort

Liability for **incitement** is exclusive to products that are expressive. This cause of action holds a defendant liable if the expression influenced someone to act in a way that caused injury to another party (*McCollum v. CBS, Inc.*, 1988). In Chapter 3, we discussed criminal incitement as a category of speech that is not protected. The civil cause of action parallels the criminal law that bars someone from inciting violence (e.g., leading a riot), but the burden of proof for civil cases is much lower.

To win a case, the plaintiff must show that: 1) the plaintiff intended to cause the action; and 2) the expression caused the action to occur (*Byers v. Edmondson*, 2002). Once again, when it comes to products that are expressive, there is a First Amendment protection that creates a higher burden on the plaintiff.

There has been a split in incitement cases when it comes to entertainment versus commercial speech. Most cases against entertainment products have failed because the products are meant to be entertainment, not intended to inspire violent actions (*Yakubowicz v. Paramount Pictures Corp.*, 1989). For example, the producers of *Natural Born Killers* were sued when two criminals were inspired by the movie to go on a drug-infused killing spree. The case was dismissed because as an entertainment product, the producers never intended for someone to copy the violence (*Byers v. Edmondson*, 2002).

Additionally, anyone who interpreted the product to be inspiring has acted in a way independent of the producer's intent; thus, there is an intervening variable that breaks the chain of causation (*McCollum v. CBS, Inc.*, 1988). Once again, there is no social science research that shows media directly causes violence. Even when people are admittedly inspired by media products, there are intervening variables such as the psychological state of the third party (*Yakubowicz v. Paramount Pictures Corp.*, 1989).

A small number of plaintiffs have been successful in bringing negligence and incitement cases. Some courts have stated that if the product is only a call for violence without storytelling, there may be liability (*Wood & Hirokawa*, 2000). As a result, speech that is purely informative has received less protection. Also, courts have been more open to holding producers liable when the speech is commercial in nature because historically there has been less protection for such speech (see Chapter 9).

For example, in 1905, Paladin Enterprise published a book titled *Hit Man: A Technical Manual for Independent Contractors*. Someone bought the book and used it to plan a murder. The victim's family sued the publisher for wrongful death. The publisher sought to have the case dismissed based on free speech protection. However, the court held that the case could proceed because the book was an instructional guide and could be seen to be aiding the crime

(*Rice v. Paladin Enterprise*, 1997). The publisher settled the case for several million dollars and agreed to destroy all copies (Kastanek, 2014).

In the 1980s, the magazine *Soldier of Fortune* was sued several times for wrongful death in instances in which hit-men were contracted through advertising in the magazine. *Soldier of Fortune* tried to have the cases removed, claiming that the First Amendment barred such suits. Courts disagreed, and cases could move forward. The magazine settled one case (*Norwood v. Soldier of Fortune Magazine*, 1987), but went to trial in another. In the trial, the magazine was found liable and had to pay $9 million (*Eimann v. Soldier of Fortune Magazine*, 1989), which eventually led to the magazine going out of business.

Note that the elements of both negligence and incitement torts are similar. Thus, plaintiffs often sue for both torts (if the state recognizes both) among other causes of action. In civil cases, attorneys often sue for several different torts to increase the chance of getting a settlement or going to trial.

Infliction of Emotional Distress

Sometimes a person's actions can be so extreme that they have a lasting psychological effect on a victim. When this happens, the law allows people to sue under the common law of **infliction of emotional distress**. The cause of action has two elements: 1) the defendant's action was extreme and outrageous; and 2) the action caused the plaintiff to suffer severe emotional distress (American Law Institute, 1965, Sec. 46). All 50 states recognize the tort when the act is intentional, but some only require it to be a negligent act (Kircher, 2007). The latter is easier to win as the plaintiff does not have to prove that the defendant meant to cause the injury, just that they were reckless. Once again, with all the elements of this tort, it is a question of fact for the jury to determine.

For intentional infliction of emotional distress, a plaintiff needs only to show severe emotional stress as there is no requirement for proof of physical symptoms, such as depression, illness, and being bed ridden (American Law Institute, 1965, Sec. 46). But courts are less likely to accept just testimony of psychological distress and will need evidence from doctors, family, and employers that the plaintiff was showing such symptoms (*Harris v. Jones*, 1977). Yet, in application, juries will often rely solely on outrageous conduct to assume distress, thus punishing for the conduct (Kircher, 2007). For negligent infliction of emotional distress, most jurisdictions require a physical manifestation of the distress (Kircher, 2007). The less outrageous the defendant's action, the more requirement there is for physical manifestations (Dobbs, 2000).

Ultimately, the emotional stress must be so severe that no reasonable person could endure it (American Law Institute, 1965, Sec. 46). But if the plaintiff has a unique vulnerability, such as a diagnosed phobia, this could rise to the level of emotional distress as any reasonable person could not bear a phobia (*Nickerson v. Hodges*, 1920). Generally, there are four categories of outrageous conduct: abuse of power, picking on a vulnerable plaintiff, continued harassment, and threatening harm. Nonetheless, it is still quite difficult for a plaintiff to prevail in cases in which the claimed injury is emotional distress.

In order for an action to be considered extreme and outrageous, it has to be "so outrageous in character, and so extreme in degree, as to go beyond all possible bounds of decency, and to be regarded as atrocious, and utterly intolerable in a civilized community" (American Law Institute, 1965, Sec. 46). This is difficult for a plaintiff to show when it comes to expression because the First Amendment allows for "breathing room" for free speech (*New York Times v. Sullivan*, 1964).

Historically, this law was usually tied to events surrounding the death of a loved one. For example, a morgue's mishandling of a deceased body may be outrageous, and surviving relatives would be quite traumatized by such an action (*Gostkowski v. Roman Catholic Church of the Sacred Hearts of Jesus & Mary*, 1933). Another example was the Westboro Baptist Church was sued for infliction of emotional distress for protesting at a funeral of soldier who was killed in Iraq. At the trial level, the church lost the case, and the jury awarded the plaintiff—the soldier's father—$9 million. But the U.S. Supreme Court overturned the case citing that the church did not aim its speech at the persons but rather at the public issue of LGBT rights, thus it was protected speech (*Snyder v. Phelps*, 2011).

In the case of *Hustler Magazine v. Falwell* (1988), the pornographic magazine ran an ad parody that targeted the Rev. Jerry Falwell, who had been a vocal critic of indecency in the media. The ad, which parodied a liquor advertisement, used double-entendres to describe the first time people tried the alcohol. But the parody made explicit claims about Falwell being drunk when he gave sermons and having his first sexual experience with his mother in an outhouse. Falwell sued the magazine for libel, invasion of privacy, and infliction of emotional distress. The lower court dismissed the libel and privacy claim, but Falwell won on the infliction of emotional distress claim. But, on appeal, the U.S. Supreme Court held that the magazine's expression was protected parody, and because Falwell was a public figure, he needed to prove actual malice in order to win. The Court's decisions to protect *Hustler Magazine* and later the Westboro Baptist Church illustrate that it is impermissible for plaintiffs to use civil lawsuits to punish speech on public affairs.

Other Forms of Harassment

Generally, when we think of **harassment**, we think of continuous, uninvited verbal or physical behavior. Legally, harassment can be a criminal violation (e.g., stalking or threats) as well as civil tort (e.g., sexual harassment or discrimination). The following examples fall under our general definition of harassment, but may not be the specific legal claim. But other torts, such as negligence, incitement, and infliction of emotional distress, have been used to sue perpetrators.

Since the beginning of the century and with the advent of the internet, cyberbullying—when people harass and intimidate online—has been a prominent concern. The issue has become of great importance for schools, although adults can be victims as well (Hegman, 2014). It has been exacerbated with the popularity of social media. In 2019, 60% of teens reported that they have been bullied. Teen suicides rose 50% in the 2010s, and some have pointed to social media bullying as being a driving force (Abbot, 2019). Teens have blamed politicians and social media for not doing enough to address the issue of cyberbullying (Anderson, 2018).

There have been several cases in which bullies were sued because their victims committed suicide. In such cases, if the bully told the victim that they should commit suicide, then it may be evidence of intent. But even in a negligence (or wrongful death) case, the plaintiff would need to prove causation, which is difficult because of the intervening variable of the action itself (Waldman, 2012).

Another form of online harassment has been **revenge porn,** in which a scorned lover publishes a sex video that was privately made when the couple was together. In the past, there were many profitable websites solely dedicated to publishing revenge porn. Attempts to remove these videos and shut down such sites was difficult because these sites were under no legal requirement to take them down. But, in the last decade, 46 states and the District of Columbia passed laws making revenge porn illegal (16 of the states have it as a misdemeanor only). Generally, these laws require a showing of an attempt to harass.

Another form of harassment is **doxing** in which someone exposes or threatens to expose online private (or semi-public) information about another person with malicious intent (Honan, 2014). It is akin to harassment and can be used to intimidate a person. But there is very little statutory protection against doxing.

Doxing is an extension of an online environment where close to 40% of people have reported experiencing some form of harassment. This number increases dramatically for female users (Duggan, 2014). A prominent example of misogyny online was Gamergate in 2014, when online trolls retaliated against high-profile women in the video game industry who had called for a greater inclusion of women (Dewey, 2014). The victims of Gamergate were harassed and eventually doxed when their addresses were made public. It got so bad for the women that they were reluctant to leave their homes as they feared for their lives (Dewey, 2014). Unfortunately for such victims, the act of doxing alone is not a crime because the information is public, and publishing is protected free speech. The only hope for doxing victims is that defendants can be charged with other crimes such as harassment, cyberstalking, or making threats.

Attempts to regulate doxing and revenge porn have run into constitutional issues because some argue that the attempts violate the First Amendment as a content-based regulation (Laird, 2019). Also, the U.S. Supreme Court has held in previous cases, third parties cannot be held liable for disseminating information attained through the independent actions of a third party (*Bartnicki v. Vopper*, 2001).

Virtual Issues in Civil Liberty

1. **Should companies be liable of contributory negligence when stored data are used for harassment?**

In 2015, a hacker group called "The Inside Group" gained access to the registry list for Ashley Madison, a website dedicated to connecting people who are interested in extramarital affairs (Lord, 2017). The hackers published the names in the database, which was previously private information. The personal consequences of the publication can have an adverse effect on someone, including depression, lethargy, and stress-induced illness. The Ashley Madison leak led to several suicides of people whose names were exposed (Segal, 2015). The hack was a criminal act as well as a violation of privacy. But, do the companies holding such information have any liability?

The person or organization that hacked the technology and published the information is certainly at risk of civil liability (as well as criminal charges). But suing them can be difficult because they have to be found. In a case of doxing or revenge porn, it might be easier to locate the perpetrator. They are certainly attempting to inflict emotional distress through their outrageous conduct of publishing the information. But when suing individuals, it might not be worth the cost of time and money because the defendant may not be able to pay the jury award.

In these cases, plaintiffs may want to sue the company that made or operates the technology for negligence (or products liability). Companies that operate connected devices have a duty of care to their customers. Also, it is foreseeable that some people will act recklessly with the company's products. A security system could be compromised and allow a secure place to be opened. For example, a car could be controlled by an outside user. If someone were to get injured by the misdeeds of a third party, a company could be held liable if it did not properly protect against the risk. But negligence is difficult to prove, unless it can be proven that the company knew or should have known (Dobbs, 2000). This is also assuming that there is only one producer, but in reality, the hardware, software, and other components of technology are often made by many different developers.

2. Will VR be treated as expressive content essentially immune to negligence cases or as a product open to liability?

After a mass shooting occurs, there is the inevitable question as to why this tragedy happened. Invariably, it is discovered that the shooter was a fan of violent video games. Thus, the narrative often becomes that video games caused the real-life violence (Jaccarino, 2015). This blame often extends to subsequent legal action (*James v. Meow Media, Inc.*, 2002). But, as mentioned before, such civil action against video games has not worked because video games are a form of expression and merely entertainment. Moreover, social science failed to show a direct causation (Salam & Stack, 2018).

But virtual reality may be different. Early studies have indicated that virtual reality technology may have stronger effects than previous video game technology (LaMotte, 2017). VR technology comes with warnings similar to other video games about seizures, dizziness, and shock. Like other games, VR can lead to addiction and even health issues, such as dehydration, obesity, and muscular attrition. However, VR technology has an inherent danger that previous technology did not—people wear eye covers and move around in virtual reality (LaMotte, 2017).

When *Pokémon Go* hit the market in 2016, it grew to be a huge sensation. The augmented-reality (AR) game, which allows users to catch cartoon characters with their phone, became extremely popular, and millions of people walked around towns looking for characters to catch. Because people look at their phones while they walk and play, some players caused incidents because they failed to pay attention to their surroundings. The game also places characters to catch on both public property and private property, potentially creating a public nuisance for private property owners overwhelmed by players (Gardner, 2017). In some cases, players trespassed to get a character.

Some users played while driving a car, which led to car accidents. Other players were so distracted that they walked into roads. One *Pokémon Go* player was reported to have walked right off a cliff (Rocha, 2016). Now, Niantic, the maker of *Pokémon Go,* has since added warnings for players to be aware of their surroundings, to avoid dangerous areas, and not to drive while playing.

But, if other AR games mimic *Pokémon Go* and enough players continue to use it in a dangerous way, there may be a push to hold the producers liable.

VR technology could also lead to negligence cases. If someone is hurt for the reasons previously noted, then the person may sue the company. Because *Pokémon Go* is an augmented reality game, the players' sight is not totally impeded. But a similar VR game could be more problematic. More than likely, a VR game would not require someone to move as far as a game like *Pokémon Go* does. But a VR sports game could have someone run some short distance, enough to create a risk (Ehrenkranz, 2016). However, when users blind themselves with the goggles, they assume the risk that they will get hurt, and that is a defense to negligence.

The question will be whether AR/VR content is treated as a service, deserving a negligence standard, or as a good, which has strict liability. Even if we assume that it is a service, will it be the same level of expression as a video game that gives users more control over the content? The possible injuries are foreseeable, and once an incident has occurred, they are no longer far-fetched. The final element of proximate cause will once again rely on effects research. It is plausible that VR technology may have stronger effects than traditional media do.

If a VR game allows avatars to have great autonomy in a game, virtual torts may be applicable in real world courts. As with criminal acts, the torts or virtual assault may be actionable. It may be easier to sue for infliction of emotional distress since outrageous conduct will have occurred. But when it is not an actual contact, then courts may require a more severe emotional distress.

3. Who should be held liable when artificial intelligence causes a personal injury?

Artificial intelligence may one day be given a great deal of autonomy. As discussed in Chapter 2, self-driving cars may fill the roads soon. Who will be responsible when a self-driving car gets into an accident? If there are still people driving alongside automated cars, then there is a chance that humans will make mistakes. So, tech companies argue that if there are only self-driving cars, then no accidents will occur. But what if there is a malfunction? Companies will not accept liability lightly and instead will look to fight it in court.

As existing technology advances, like with self-driving cars, it seems likely that the law will be an extension of current products liability. There is strict liability for a product that has a design flaw. If a manufacturer puts out a product that is unsafe, the firm will be held liable. For example, if the injury is caused by the action of the self-driving car, and the injury was foreseeable, the company that designed it or controls it will be liable (Bradshaw, 2018).

If the car's passengers are injured, they may sue the car company. But if another driver or pedestrian is hurt, they may be able to sue the passengers (if they own the car) as well as the car company. Passengers also may be able to then sue the car company, assuming the owner did not intervene and use the car in a way that it was not supposed to be used (e.g., change the AI coding).

If the AI decided to save the pedestrian, but in doing so, hurt the passengers, then the equation is different. If it were a human driver, a court may have applied a reasonable person standard. But that standard will have to be analyzed when it comes to AI. If AI surpasses human reasoning, its choice may be considered to always be reasonable, thus no liability.

If AI is constantly learning and updating, at some point it will move beyond the original manufacturer's input. If the action was a new learned behavior, the liability may shift to the AI. Machines, as goods, fall under strict liability, whereas actions by people fall under negligence. But, for advanced AI, there will be questions of whether it is legally a machine or a person, and what level of liability will be applied.

The questions change when we move beyond purely consumer products to communication technology, for example, when a bot makes a threat. In Amsterdam, police questioned a man after his Twitter bot tweeted, "I seriously want to kill people" (Weaver, 2015). For criminal liability, the state would have to show an intent to make a threat. But this clearly was not the case. In a civil case, with a lower burden of proof, a plaintiff may be able to sue in a jurisdiction that recognizes negligent infliction of emotional distress or assault for such a threat aimed at someone.

With AI, it seems unreasonable that it would behave in a negligent manner because it would be designed not to do so. But as mentioned above, machines can glitch. Moreover, it would be difficult to imagine AI would have the intent to incite violent acts or to cause emotional distress. However, as discussed in Chapter 3, bots are currently being used to spread hate speech, and AI is learning language from humans who often speak in offensive ways. Thus, AI could learn from humans to spread vicious messages. Once again, if it is part of the design for a bot, then there is a human party who can be sued. But if it is learned behavior for a smart machine, then we may have to turn to suing robots.

CASE STUDY
Virtual Worlds, Real Life Crime

In the summer of 2014, a disturbing story was in the headlines. Two 14-year-old girls had lured their classmate into the woods and attempted to murder her with a knife. The victim was stabbed two dozen times. Fortunately, she escaped and found help. She survived, and the perpetrators were quickly apprehended.

What made this story unique—beyond its heinousness—was that during the interrogation, the perpetrators revealed their motive for the crime: Slender Man. The girls were fanatics for this online meme. One of the girls even claimed that the Slender Man had visited her and had told her that if she murdered someone, she could go and live with him forever (Killelea, 2017).

The online meme is just a story. It started as photoshopped images of a long faceless man who was bright white and dressed in a black suit. The legend was that the Slender Man appeared in photos of children right before they went missing because he was the one who took them. None of this was true. It was just a modern-day boogie-man story meant to entertain by scaring people. But for these girls, who undoubtedly had psychological issues, it was much more than a story.

People being inspired by what they see in the media is not a new issue. But the legal cases that have arisen have come from passive media platforms. Slender Man was mostly text on an online site. The site also had some photoshopped pictures, a movie, and a video game, so still mostly traditional technology. But what might happen if such stories move to more immersive platforms? What if the Slender Man story occurred in a virtual reality platform, and players called on other players to commit violence? Would the producers still be free from liability?

Discussion Questions

1. To what degree do violent stories have a greater effect on people if they are told through virtual reality?

2. Should violent content in virtual reality be regulated? Why or why not?

3. To what extent, if any, should a creator of a violent story be held liable for the actions of the audience?

4. If a VR story is like the Slender Man and calls for the audience to be a proxy, should the creator be held liable? Why or why not?

CHAPTER 7

Obscenity and Violent Content

I n 2018, the U.S. House of Representatives passed the Curbing Realistic Exploitative Electronic Pedophilic Robots (CREEPER) Act. This act was aimed at blocking the sale of "anatomically-correct doll[s], mannequin[s], or robot[s], with the features of, or with features that resemble those of, a minor, intended for use in sexual acts" (Sec. 3).

The supporters of the bill argue that such dolls promote sexual abuse of children and that they "not only lead to rape, but they make rape easier by teaching the rapist about how to overcome resistance and subdue the victim" (CREEPER Act, 2018, Sec. 2). Supporters believe that the dolls could be a gateway that would corrupt users and normalize pedophilia ("Congress Wants," 2018).

Critics of the bill argue that the dolls are, at worst, a victimless crime and that there is no scientific evidence that they lead to an actual crime. Moreover, critics say that the dolls could even be cathartic for people who may have such tendencies, but there is no evidence of either benefits or harms. Ultimately, they find it to be an encroachment by the government on an individual's freedom ("Congress Wants," 2018). As of the end of 2019, the federal bill has yet to become law, but several states have passed their own version of the law.

These dolls are an example of how people can use new technologies for sex, sometimes to fulfill deviant desires. This should be no surprise as our pop culture is inundated with depictions of such sex and violence, so it is only natural that these types of uses will spread to new technologies as they emerge. But with traditional media, the audience is detached from depictions

of sexual fantasies. With newer technologies, our fantasies may be indistinguishable from reality. So, the question is: How should we regulate fantasies
of sex and violence?

This chapter examines how emerging media could be used for sex and
violence. The chapter outlines contemporary regulation of sex and violence
followed by virtual issues related to emerging media.

Legal Principles in Obscenity and Violent Content

History of Regulating Sexual Depictions

The U.S. Supreme Court has had a muddled history when it comes to defining
obscenity. There was very little evolution of obscenity law in the first 150
years of the nation, and the laws were quite draconian. Basically, anything
found to be offensive was obscene, including discussions about birth control
and abortion. If the material was thought to have a negative effect on children,
then it could be deemed to be illegal (Dennis, 2007).

In *Roth v. United States* (1957), the U.S. Supreme Court held that, although
obscenity was outside the protection of the First Amendment, some depictions
of sex could be protected if they had redeeming value. However, the Court
was still unclear as to what that meant. A few years later, in *Jacobellis v. Ohio*
(1964), Justice Lewis Powell famously defined obscenity as "he knows when
he sees it." This obviously made it difficult to determine when something was
obscene as the defendant would not know until a judge determined it to be so.

Current Legal Test for Obscenity

The U.S. Supreme Court made it a little clearer in the case of *Miller v. California*
(1972). Miller had been arrested for violating the California obscenity statute
by mailing graphic advertisements for his pornography shop to unwilling
recipients. In deciding the case, the U.S. Supreme Court rejected the "social
redeeming value" test and laid out a new legal test for obscenity:

> (1) [W]hether the average person, applying contemporary commu-
> nity standards would find that the work, taken as a whole, appeals
> to the prurient interest; (2) whether the work depicts or describes,
> in a patently offensive way, sexual conduct specifically defined
> by the applicable state law; and (3) whether the work taken as a
> whole, lacks serious literary, artistic, political or scientific value.
> (*Miller v. California*, p. 24)

The first prong of the Miller test says that in order to be obscene, the speech
has to be sexual in nature. There have been attempts to apply the Miller test to

depictions of violence, but the U.S. Supreme Court has overturned legislative attempts to just simply replace the word sex with violence (*Brown v. Entertainment Merchants Association*, 2011). For example, a federal law banning the sale of depictions of animal abuse mirrored the Miller test. The U.S. Supreme Court overturned the law stating that it was overbroad and not parallel to unprotected obscenity (*United States v. Stevens*, 2010).

The second prong examines obscenity as a local norm. These "community standards" of obscenity can vary across the nation and are usually dictated by a statute. But the variation in community standards is trumped by the national standard of the third prong of the Miller test. Known as the **SLAPS test** (serious literary, artistic, political, or scientific value), this prong requires courts to consider how the work would be assessed throughout the country (*Pope v. Illinois*, 1987). So, even though a work may violate the community standards in Nebraska, it will still be protected if it would be considered artistic in New York City.

The Miller test is a better alternative to the previous tests because it gives more instruction and allows more freedom of speech. But the contemporary test still has issues. It is quite long and filled with many ambiguous words such as "prurient," "offensive," and "serious." Definitions of what is considered "sexual in nature" can be divergent across the United States (Creasy, 2010). The test also requires for works to be examined on the whole, rather than one page or scene, theoretically allowing for works to contain obscene parts. This ambiguity—seen as flexibility by some—has made obscenity cases difficult to prosecute. Thus, since the 1970s, obscenity cases have all but disappeared in the United States (Adler, 2001). Despite calls of new policy to fight moral degradation, generally the courts have supported a legal framework that if a person does not like the material, "then avert your eyes." Ultimately, material can be considered obscene if: 1) it has a sexual appeal; 2) it violates community standards; and 3) lacks any serious value.

Per Se Obscenity: Child Pornography

Generally, in the United States, most material that is sexual in nature is protected. When the action involves consenting adults and in a private setting, there is very little chance of it being stopped for legal reasons (*Lawrence v. Texas*, 2003). As a result, there are very few obscenity prosecutions in the United States.

The one significant exception is child pornography, which is patently illegal. These types of depictions are so abhorrent that convicted child pornographers receive mandated sentences. If ever released, they also must spend the rest of their lives on a public sex offender's registry and must report this to their neighbors (Vinyard, 2016).

The U.S. Supreme Court has held that whatever artistic value that child pornography might contain is heavily outweighed by the negative effect that it has on its victims. In addition, the Court has stated that allowing people to own such content will whet the appetite of pedophiles and incentivize the creation of more child pornography. Thus, more children would be victimized (*New York v. Ferber*, 1982).

Child pornography involves persons who are minors. For federal law, Congress defines a minor as under 18 years old. At the state level, about half of the laws define the age of majority as 17 years old. The other states are split between 16 and 18 years old. In half of the states, sexual partners can have age differences, even if one is a minor. The laws range between 2 to 5 years difference, with Utah allowing up to a 10-year difference (Howe, n.d.).

Virtual Child Pornography

With the rise of the internet came a parallel rise in pornography. The new digital technology also enabled the manipulation of videos and photos. One of the major concerns was that technology would lead to a rise in child pornography as well. So, in 1996, Congress passed the Child Pornography Protection Act (CPPA) that extended the child pornography laws to the internet. But the CPPA also barred any depictions that "appeared to be a minor" engaged in sexual activity. This included manipulated images of real children, but also depictions of fictional child-like characters, including animation. The law did not require proof that the depiction was of a minor, just that it could be interpreted as being a minor.

The pornography industry decided to challenge the CPPA as being overly broad. The industry, which has thrived on the internet, includes some content with actors who look like minors. The government counter-argued that the virtual pornography law had the same justification as other child pornography laws: the speech has little value, it whets the appetite of pedophiles, and creates a market for real child pornography.

In *Ashcroft v. Free Speech Coalition* (2002), the U.S. Supreme Court overturned the CPPA as unconstitutional. The Court stated that the arts have been fascinated with teenage sexuality for a long time, citing classic works such as Shakespeare's *Romeo and Juliet*. The Court noted that the CPPA would outlaw many works of protected entertainment, including movies that had won Oscars. The Court also said that there is no evidence that the virtual pornography leads to pedophilia or the creation of real child pornography.

The Court did provide some answers for legislatures. It said that for a fictional work to be prohibited, it would have to fail the Miller test. The U.S. Congress responded by passing the PROTECT Act of 2003, which allows virtual child pornography to be punished if a jury finds it to be obscene.

Under the PROTECT Act, a defendant who is found guilty is considered a child pornographer and must register as a sex offender. The PROTECT Act has been challenged several times, but courts have continued to uphold its constitutionality. For example, in 2008, an Iowa man pleaded guilty under the PROTECT Act for possessing Japanese comics that depicted bestiality and pedophilia. He served six months in prison and underwent psychological treatment (*United States v. Handley*, 2008).

Indecency

Most sexual material does not rise to the level of obscenity; thus, it is legal. For example, pornography is rarely considered to be obscene because it has some social and artistic value. However, sexual material can be regulated through **indecency** regulations. Thus, pornography cannot air on certain media at certain times and be accessible to certain audiences.

One of the only platforms that is regulated for indecency is broadcast radio and television. The indecency regulations for these two media began with their commercialization in the 1920s. The Radio Act of 1927 dictated that the airwaves were a public good. Thus, radio (and later television) stations are licensed and have to serve the public interest. Part of this public interest requirement is a prohibition on obscene and indecent material, including sexual acts, nudity, and vulgarities. The Radio Act of 1927 and the Communications Act of 1934 prohibit the government from censoring broadcasters, but the FCC can fine a licensed station that airs indecent content. Multiple offenses can lead to a station losing its license.

Until the 1970s, broadcasters self-censored by employing 'censors' to review scripts, as a result, the FCC rarely received public complaints. But in the 1970s, content on the airwaves changed with more depictions of sex and uses of vulgarities. In 1973, a New York City radio station, WBAI-FM, aired in the middle of the afternoon a small segment of George Carlin's monologue on the "seven dirty words" that cannot be said on television. The FCC received a complaint and warned the station not to do it again. Although the station was not fined, it decided to appeal the case to challenge the constitutionality of the FCC's indecency regulations.

The U.S. Supreme Court upheld the indecency regulations for broadcasting. The Court reiterated that the broadcast airwaves were a public good and that licensees had to serve the public interest. The Court also stated that the airwaves were pervasive, and children and unwilling adults could not avoid them. Finally, the Court stated that the law was not a complete ban because the FCC allowed for safe harbor hours from 10 p.m.–6 a.m. (*FCC v. Pacifica Foundation*, 1978).

A quarter of a century later, the television and radio industry had changed greatly. Most people received their programming through paid subscriptions rather than over-the-air broadcasting. Much of the programming was consumed on demand with time-shifting and place-shifting. The culture had also become much more tolerant of public displays of sexuality and the use of vulgarities. So, in the early 2000s, when the FCC fined the broadcast stations for using fleeting expletives (a vulgarity that slips on live unscripted programming), the broadcasting companies attempted to challenge the constitutionality of the FCC's indecency laws.

Once again, the U.S. Supreme Court refused to overturn the indecency rules. Instead, it claimed that the rules were too vague, thus violating the broadcasters' due process rights. The FCC was forced to go back and draft clearer rules (FCC v. FOX Television Stations).

However, as of 2020, they FCC has not clarified the indecency rules. It is likely the FCC will not forward any amended regulations because the media environment has changed so much (Gardner, 2019b). In general, as long as broadcast stations do not show sex that includes nudity or use the f-word before 10 p.m., then it is acceptable.

There were several attempts to have indecency rules for the internet. In 1996, Congress passed the Communications Decency Act, which would have brought indecency rules to the internet in the same manner as in broadcasting media. However, the U.S. Supreme Court ruled that the indecency rules as applied to the internet were unconstitutional. The Court stated that the internet would be given broad protections more akin to print media than to broadcasting (*Reno v. American Civil Liberties Union*, 1997). Congress tried again in 1998 to block minors' access to indecency online by passing the Children Online Protection Act. But once again the U.S. Supreme Court struck down the law as unconstitutional (*Ashcroft v. American Civil Liberties Union*, 2002).

Regulating Violent Content

In the United States, there is a long history of regulating depictions of sex. But depictions of violence have been less regulated. In general, it has been much easier to find depictions of violence in U.S. media, from television shows to movies to video games (Davis, 2015). As Justice Scalia noted in *Brown v. Entertainment Merchant Association* (2011), humans have long had a fascination with violence including in the fairy tales told to children.

With the advent of any new media, there is usually social panic about its effect on youth (Herrman, 2017). Video games have suffered the same fate. Over the last two decades there has been a rise in mass shootings, specifically in schools. Invariably, it seems that authorities discover that the perpetrator was obsessed with violent video games. After such terrible incidents, people want simple answers, and citing video games as the cause has been a popular answer (Disis, 2018).

As a result, many states passed laws prohibiting the sale of video games to minors. The video game industry challenged California's law, and in 2011, the U.S. Supreme Court deemed it to be unconstitutional (*Brown v. Entertainment Merchant Association*, 2011). The Court held that video games were a form of speech and that such a ban was a content-based regulation. The Court said that the State of California could not prove that violent video games caused acts of violence justifying such a law. The Court also said that the law had a chilling effect on producers. Finally, the majority argued that it should be left to parents to decide if their children should have such games. Ultimately, the Court stated that violent depictions will not be treated like sexual obscenities.

Today, most platforms are free from indecency regulation, but still choose to self-regulate. The Motion Picture Association of America (MPAA) has used a rating system since 1968 (G, PG, PG-13, R, NC-17) while television broadcasting, cable, and streaming use a slightly different rating system (TV-Y, TV-7, TV-14, TV-MA). The Entertainment Software Ratings Board provides ratings for video games (E, E 10+, T, M, A 18+). The internet does not use ratings, but pornographic sites will often ask the user's age (meaning that the user needs to be able to do the math) ("Content Rating," n.d.). The ratings system designation for mature content considers depictions of both sex and violence. Depictions of sex will get stricter ratings quicker than depictions of violence will. For example, most superhero movies are PG-13. The MPAA will allow for brief nudity, but not sexual activity. However, depictions of violence are allowed, so long as it is not too realistic *and* persistent (Buchanan, 2016).

Virtual Issues in Obscenity and Violence in Emerging Media

1. **How will people who use connected devices for intimate purposes be protected?**

Online pornography is big business with revenues of $3 billion a year (Booten, 2015). About 5% of all registered websites are dedicated to pornography with the most popular pornography sites receiving millions of visits per month. Estimates of web traffic for pornography range between 10 to 15% of all traffic, though some claims are as high as 30%. Much of that consumption is done through phones, with some estimates that 20% of mobile downloads are for pornography (Castleman, 2016). These numbers speak to people's strong desire to consume the content.

For most people, consumption of pornography is innocuous and sometimes beneficial to their lives. Although sexual activity among consenting adults is legal, most people do not share this information with others. Most consumption of pornography is in the privacy of their homes.

But if pornography is consumed with a connected device, there may be a concern about who is watching. Information about sexual activity is collected by providers and is at risk of being shared publicly. The sites use cookies to track people and individualize the content offerings on their platforms. Thus, the information is saved and stored. The traffic is also on a public network meaning that it can be followed. For example, NSA whistleblower Edward Snowden claimed that the agency was tracking the viewing habits of suspicious "radicalized" Muslims in the hope to catch them viewing pornography so that it could discredit them (Greenwald et al., 2013).

What is certainly true is that when we download apps or use smart technology, we agree to their terms of service. The terms may include allowing them to access and upload our photos and videos, listen to our voices, and access our devices' cameras (Komando, 2015). If these devices are always on waiting to be used, then it could be recording such private moments.

It is well known that people should be careful about the photos and videos they take and send, but the technology may also allow cameras and microphones to be accessed through backchannels—thus, recording without our knowledge. For example, whistleblowers have exposed that the government could access and use cameras and microphones in the devices, including viewing people in private moments (Schneier, 2013).

Individuals will have to rely on the power of tech companies to stop third parties from accessing these devices (Sleyukh, 2016). But even when the providers work diligently to protect the information, hackers may get the information and share it with the public. In 2014, Jennifer Lawrence, Rhianna, and Kate Upton were among several celebrities who were victims of an Apple phone hack through a phishing scam. In Lawrence's case, the hacker took and distributed nude photos she had taken privately and never shared with anyone (Darrah, 2018). The hacker was eventually discovered and sentenced, but the photos had already been seen by millions (O'Malley, 2017).

Thus, technology producers will have to invest millions of dollars into securing such devices and apps. For example, Amazon Alexa has many safeguards to make sure that any recordings it may store happens after the device gains explicit consent from the speaker (Weisbaum, 2017). But even with today's advanced technology, it has been difficult to stop hackers. When the hack is an attempt to steal credit cards, the cost is absorbed by the hacked company, which it can pay back (or not charge the individual) and collect insurance (Yakowicz, 2015). When the hacker reveals intimate moments, then it will be difficult to make the person whole again. Companies may instead place a waiver in the terms of agreement stating that they are not liable for any collection of information by a third party.

2. Will virtual reality increase the negative effects of pornographic and violent content?

The pornography industry is often the first to use new technology. Pornography was an early genre in books, movies and the internet (Ewalt, 2018). Today, the pornography industry is leading the way into uses for virtual reality. Some predictions are that by 2025, one-third of all VR content will be pornography (Booten, 2015).

VR content is the next step in the evolution of traditional media such as television, movies, and video games. The genres and products will be similar to traditional content, but more immersive. So, for pornography, this means content that makes the scenes seem as real as possible, including connecting the content to other technology, such as wearable **haptic gear**, which simulates physical touch, or syncing content to a sex toy (Breslin, 2018).

More than likely, VR pornography will be another extension of the industry that will make it more fulfilling for users. But there are some concerns that the more immersive the pornography, the more likely it will cause addiction and begin to replace real-life sex. Such addiction can be harmful to real-life relationships (Griffiths, 2016). The issue of pornography addiction is not new—some estimate that in 50% of divorces, a male partner was accused of having an online pornography addiction (Castleman, 2016).

Each new medium often brings along new social panic. Parent groups have advocated for ratings on video games, as well as for other media such as music (Schonfeld, 2015). Legislators have pushed for bans on video game sales to minors (*Brown v. Entertainment Merchants Association*, 2011). When it comes to professionally produced VR, it will likely follow the self-regulation of the established media industries (e.g., NC-17 ratings). Most of those games and videos will probably avoid hardcore sexuality to garner a rating for mass appeal. But, as with contemporary media, violence can be quite extreme, ubiquitous, and gratuitous without getting an unmarketable rating (Abrams, 2018).

Moreover, videos games that are shared on the internet are not rated. Thus, these games can have extreme violence and sex. Games traded on the **dark net**—a network of encrypted sites not available through commercial search engines—could have such depictions and go under the radar. In 2015, a game called *Sad Satan* was supposedly discovered on the dark web (Gonzalez, 2015). The game had pictures of violent criminals, satanic imagery, and cryptic messages. Such games would be outside the self-regulation of the industry.

3. Will robots replace humans in the sex industry?

Sex machines have been around for centuries (Frucci, 2010). These days, the sex toy market is a $15 billion a year industry (Burns, 2016). As part of that market, companies sell dolls that are meant to look like humans, though no one would mistake them for real. The next step is to make the dolls into automatons. Although there are already legal attempts to block the sale of sex robots, for the most part they are not yet a mass commercial product.

As previously discussed , VR content can be hooked up to haptic gear to simulate the physical touch, but a robot would provide the physical stimulus. Moreover, if it were indistinguishable from a real person, then the robot could meet other needs like love and companionship, which are not provided by simple machines. If there is already concern about the impact that online pornography can have on relationships, then the fear of sex robots far sur-passing that concern is foreseeable.

One argument in favor of sex robots is that they can replace humans as sex workers, an occupation that has historically operated illegally and created dangerous environments for workers. In the early years of the technology, it will probably be too expensive for individual ownership of robots. As with other expensive technology, it is often public businesses that offer affordable access to it. The same is true with access to robots. In Toronto, Ontario, and Houston, Texas, brothels are already offering sex robots to the public. Unsurprisingly, there is public concern (Dougherty, 2018). Even though it may be offensive to some, for brothels owners, using robots may be preferred as they removes issues about abuse and disease. Also, robots do not require any pay or benefits. Currently, prostitution laws do not include robots, so it is difficult to stop a brothel from offering them. A town could try to zone sexually oriented businesses in remote locations only or attempt to shut them down as a public nuisance.

CASE STUDY
Sexual Deviance in Virtual Worlds

In 2016, a woman, who uses the pseudonym "Jordan Belamire," was playing the virtual reality game *QuiVr* on an HTC Vive VR system. She had played the game many times before and enjoyed it. But this time was different. While she was playing, another player by the name BigBro442 started grabbing the breasts and crotch of her avatar. Belamire, who had been sexually assaulted twice in real life, said the virtual assault left the same emotional pain as an actual assault. In response, QuiVR updated the code to give players a personal bubble (Buchleitner, 2018).

A North Carolina mother was astounded to find that her 7-year-old daughter who played the game *Roblox,* a game with a target audience of children, was assaulted by another avatar. She claimed that her daughter's avatar was being gang-raped on a playground in the game. She reported the incident to the producers of the game, and they were working on preventing such instances in the future (Seeley, 2018).

Entire virtual worlds exist in games like *Sims, Second Life*, and *Roblox*. In these games, players can create avatars with the only limits being the programming and their imagination. None of the most popular games allow sexual activity in their virtual worlds. But, as mentioned above, a few have seen such incidences occur.

But there are several pornographic VR games in existence, including some that are online multiplayer games. In these games, users can act out most sexual fantasies. Players can create avatars that resemble real people, people of their imagination, or even fantastic beings that barely resemble humans.

The examples mentioned offer instances of virtual assault on avatars, including a player who was a young child. The perpetrator may not have known that the player was a child. In these games, the avatars are pixelated characters with no discernible age. But, in other games, the graphics are more advanced, and the avatars are more realistic. In a more realistic game, a sexual assault would be even more appalling, and attributes like age, gender, and even appearance would be known. If the users were wearing haptic technology attached to the VR, the assault could move from being virtual to being too realistic.

As in the cases above, more than likely VR producers would self-regulate their games to ensure they have commercial appeal. But, what about independent games created by individuals and not sold on a mass market. Maybe these games are never made public or maybe are traded on the dark web. A person could create a game to play out their secret fantasies, including deviant ones such as rape, incest, pedophilia, necrophilia, and bestiality.

Discussion Questions

1. Should people be allowed to play out sexual fantasies in virtual worlds? If so, should there be any limits?

2. To what extent should the government be able to prosecute those who act out deviant sexual acts in virtual worlds?

3. Should the punishment be equal to a real-life crime? Why or why not?

CHAPTER 8

Intellectual Property and Identity Rights

Technology helps artists bring their ideas to life. From the simple word processor on a computer to advanced CGI technology, if artists can dream it, they can make it. The technology has been a tool to help humans develop their ideas, but the humans have been the genesis of the creativity. However, things might be changing.

Author Robin Sloan published a book using AI software he had developed by having the machine study already published works in order to learn how to write. He typed in lines such as, "The bison are gathered around the canyon." Then the software would generate new sentences based on what it had learned. The AI wrote, "The bison are gathered around the canyon by the bare sky" (Streitfeld, 2018, para. 5). This output is a bit more poetic than the input. But ultimately, it is not that impressive. Instead, what if the AI were designed to move beyond prose to learn the actual voice of a specific author. Botnik Studios designed an AI to write like J.K. Rowling, and it created a new chapter of *Harry Potter*. The program used a predictive keyboard to help fans create sentences to submit to the final project that it produced (Beck, 2017). The result was fan fiction that was meant to be in the "voice" of the original author.

All art is derivative; artists are inspired by those who came before them. But derivatives are also protected by copyright law. Fans who write fiction based on the characters in *Star Wars* or *Star Trek* are violating copyright law. The characters belong to the original authors (or their companies), no matter how much ownership the fans feel. When people are inspired by other artists, that too can be a copyright infringement if the work is too similar to the original, even if the copy is meant to be an homage.

Advanced AI will be able to produce new works by learning from previous writing, just as humans do. But, if it takes on the voice of an author like J.K Rowling or Stephen King, it could be a copyright infringement. Inspiration is important to the proliferation of the arts and generally protected because artistic output is usually an amalgam of many predecessors. But, with AI created to learn from established authors, then it seems like it was created to violate copyright. Maybe if an AI learns from reading Shakespeare or Dickens, whose works are in the public domain, then it would not be a copyright issue. But then there is the thornier question of who owns the copyright to the new work. Did the AI simply reproduce a dead author's work, or was it being inspired to be original and creative?

This chapter examines how advancements in technology can affect the laws over our creative ideas and identity. First, it discusses contemporary law for intellectual property law and identity rights, which share similar elements and defenses. Second, it investigates how issues with emerging technology could affect our property rights over our creative works and identity.

Legal Principles in IP and Identity Rights

History of Property Law

There are two main categories of property in law: real and personal. **Real property** is the tangible items that cannot be moved such as land. **Personal property** is the items that we own and can be moved (Render, 2017). Most people are familiar with the rules of real and personal property because we own lots of things such as phones, cars, clothes, and so forth. We know we can do as we please with our property, such as sell it, rent it, lend it, give it, and destroy it.

A third category of property law is **intellectual property** (IP) that protects the ideas that led to many of the consumer products we buy. It is more akin to personal property in that it can move. But, unlike personal property, it is intangible; thus, it is harder to protect. Moreover, unlike the other categories of property, IP can be consumed by many people at once without losing its value.

Nonetheless, the ownership rights for IP are not that different from other property rights. IP rights holders can do whatever they choose with the rights. Owners can sell the rights, license the rights, give away the rights, or choose not to protect the rights. They can also protect their intellectual property and sue others who use it without permission.

Patents and Trademarks

IP is divided into three broad categories: patents, trademarks, and copy-rights. Products are often protected in all three areas. For example, a phone has patented technology, trademarked aesthetics, and copyrighted content embedded. Copyright and patent protections do not last forever, but trademarks can if kept in use.

Patents are plans for an invention such as a self-driving car, 3-D printer, or a drone. For patents, the work needs to be filed with the government in order to have protection. In the United States, protection is governed by the U.S. Patent and Trademark Office and can be granted for 20 years. This period gives the patent holder exclusive rights over the product, allowing the person to profit beyond the costs of research and development (Nguti, 1986). Once the term is up, then the product enters the public domain for all to use.

Trademarks are the identifying marks used by companies, including names, slogans, and colors. Trademarks can get common law protection once in use but will have greater protection if they are filed with the government. Trademarks can be retained forever, as long as they are used actively. It is the responsibility of a company to enforce its trademark and make sure it is not being used by another company or the public generally. A company can sue another company in the same industry for trademark infringement, if it can show that customers would likely be confused about whom or what the trademark represents. A Trademark holder can sue for trademark dilution for any use that would lessen the company's association with its product.

Copyright Law

Copyrights protect "all original works of authorship fixed in tangible medium of expression" (Subject Matter of Copyright, 2012). This includes a vast array of works from stories to songs to games to architecture to speeches. But copyright protection does have it limits. For example, scriptwriters have a copyright over the completed script, but overriding themes within the script are not protected. So, a movie about magicians who study at a school of magic is not in and of itself protected. However, using names like Harry Potter or terms such as Muggles or Quidditch (or something similar sound-ing) would be a violation. Historical facts cannot be copyrighted. Hence, another scripted movie about the rock band Queen could be made, but if it were called *Bohemian Rhapsody* and used the same movie dialog, it could be a violation. Conversely, simple creations, even if not very creative, can receive protection. For example, a dictionary is a just collection of definitions in alphabetical order. But the work is protected because the creators make original choices about font, color, design, and so forth.

Over the last century, copyright law has turned into more of an economic right (Lessig, 2005). Owners of copyright have strict control over their work—they can sell it, rent it, bequeath it, and so forth. They also control use of the work including recordings, sales, displays, performances, copies, and so forth. So, it is important to know who owns a work and can control its use. This is often the person who created it. If more than one person created the work, then all persons have an equal right to the work. Thus, a co-author cannot sell the complete rights to the work, but can pass on his or her own rights. However, the original creators may not hold the rights if they are a "work for hire," such as an employee, or they have signed a contract giving away all rights. This is quite common in the entertainment industry as a sale of rights is often boilerplate language in contracts signed with studios (McDonald, 2018).

Types of Rights in Copyright Law

Derivatives: a right to any adaptations of the work

Reproduction: a right to make copies of the work

Performance: a right to perform the work live or through media

Display: a right to publicly display the work, including through media

Distribution: a right to make the work available for rent, lease, sale, etc.

TERMS OF PROTECTION

As long as a work is original and placed on a medium, it will receive copyright protection upon creation, although the creator can file with the government for extra statutory protections (Subject Matter of Copyright, 2012). The work will receive protection for a limited time after creation. In the early days of the United States, the government copied British copyright law and gave creators 14 years protection with the option of another 14 years after that. During the 20th century the length of protection was extended three times (U.S. Copyright Office, n.d.).

Currently, the duration of the copyright is 70 years after the death of the creator (Duration of Copyright, 2011). This term is set even if the copyright is licensed or sold to another entity. If a 25 year old recording artist were to live to be 100 years old, his or her body of work would not go into the public domain until late in the 22nd century. But for most commercial entertainment successes, the rights are owned by a corporation. For corporate rights holder the duration is 90 years from publication (Duration of Copyright, 2011).

Although the length of terms seems set, it may not be permanent. The last extension of copyright terms came in 1998 with the Copyright Term Extension Act (CTEA), when Congress added another 20 years. The extension was challenged by companies that use works in the public domain and wanted more works available to them. The U.S. Supreme Court upheld the extension, stating that the U.S. Constitution requires only a set limit, but does not dictate how long it should be. Justice Ginsburg, writing for the majority, felt that the term was reasonable because people now live longer and should be able to bear the fruit of their labors (*Eldred v. Ashcroft*, 2003).

The lobbyists supporting CTEA were Hollywood studios that faced losing their financial protection over their copyrights. The most significant lobbyist was The Walt Disney Company. Its Steamboat Willie version of Mickey Mouse, which was created in 1928, was slated to go into the public domain in 2004. Now that 20 years have passed since CTEA was enacted, Mickey Mouse is again set to become public domain in a few years. If Disney and others are successful, they could lobby Congress to add more years of copyright protections (Lee, 2018). As long as there is an eventual expiration, then an extension could be upheld. But corporations live in perpetuity, and they will always have the incentive to seek continuous extensions.

Once the protection term ends, then the work goes into the public domain. At that point it can be used by anyone for any purpose (Khana, 2014). As a result, using works from Shakespeare or classical music does not need to be cleared, although using recorded performances of those works by modern actors or orchestras does need to be cleared. But most works of the 20th century are still protected. The irony is that many of those works were built off works that were already in the public domain. Most famously, Walt Disney used fairy tales such as Snow White, Sleeping Beauty, and Cinderella to create his empire. Today, Disney has a copyright over its version of those fairy tales, but not the fairy tales themselves. However, Congress can change the copyright laws and place works that are already in the public domain back under copyright protection if it retroactively changes the length of terms (*Golan v. Holder*, 2012).

COPYRIGHT VIOLATIONS

There are three types of violations of copyright: piracy, infringement, and derivative use. Piracy is outright copying and distribution of a protected work. This clearly violates copyright law but has become an extensive problem in the digital age. The entertainment industry estimates that piracy costs over $50 billion a year in lost revenue, although numbers of lost sales are difficult to calculate (Raustiala & Sprigman, 2012). Despite declining numbers in online piracy due to growing streaming, **cyberlockers**, which are online file sharing services, containing illegal content are still prevalent and are difficult to stop, because as soon as one is taken down, another one pops up (Tyson, 2018).

A more controversial issue is when user-generated content on social media contains parts of copyrighted work. Under the Digital Millennium Copyright Act (1998), third-party providers, such as Facebook and YouTube, must monitor their sites for possible copyright infringement. If they do not, the third-party site can be sued for **contributory infringement**. However, some critics argue that in an attempt to comply with the law, social media sites have become too cautious and force users to take down content without considering the users' legal defenses (McMullen, 2015). But, in 2015, the Ninth Circuit court of appeals held that companies need to consider possible "fair use" before issuing a takedown notice (*Lenz v. Universal Music Corporation*, 2015).

Copyright infringement is when a creative work is too similar to another established work. This can be intentional copying to try to profit off another established work. For example, the producers of the movie *The Purge* were sued for copyright infringement. Writer Douglas Jordan-Benel claimed that he conceived the original idea and shared it with his talent agency, which then gave the script to another one of its clients who reworked the script for the film (Gardner, 2019a). The parties settled out of court.

Copyright infringement can be unintentional as well. This is common in the music industry because there are only so many notes, rhythms, beats, and so forth. For example, recording artist Sam Smith was sued by Tom Petty over the hit song "Stay with Me." Tom Petty argued that the song was too similar to his 1980s "I Won't Back Down." The two artists settled, and Tom Petty was given credits on the song (Kreps, 2015). Katy Perry was sued when a Christian rap band claimed her song "Dark Horse" was too close to the band's song "Joyful Noise"—a song Perry had claimed to never have heard (Hobson & McMahon, 2019). Perry lost her case at trial because a jury found the songs to be similar. But the award was overturned on appeal as a judge ruled the original song was not distinctive enough (Associated Press, 2020).

Copyright holders also hold rights over **derivatives** such as compilations, translation, and other ancillary works such as guides and summaries (Exclusive Rights in Copyrighted Works, 2011). The right to make sequels and prequels also belongs to the original creators, even if they have not yet thought of it. A fan may come up with a cool idea for a sequel, but they cannot create it if the work is protected by copyright.

Defenses to Copyright Infringement

Generally, no one can use any part of a copyrighted work without the expressed consent of the owner. Today, much of the use of video and audio works is allowed because the distributors have bought licenses from the major publishers. Broadcasting, satellite, and streaming services pay billions of dollars in license fees annually to use parts of works or air them in their entirety. Netflix alone paid $15 billion in licenses in 2019 (Beers, 2020). In fact, any venue that uses copyrighted work must pay a license fee, including stadiums, restaurants, and bars.

The major exception to copyright infringement is a **fair use** of a work (Limitations on Exclusive Rights, 2011). This statutory protection allows others to use a work so long as it is a limited use. In many ways, it is the free speech exception to the monopoly given to copyright holders. Just as copyright law protects authors in order to "promote the progress of the arts and sciences," fair use allows some breathing room in the use of copyright material.

To determine fair use, courts will apply a four-part test:

1. *What is the nature of the copyrighted work?*

    Generally, the newer the work, the more protection it has. The idea is that the creator has yet to fully take advantage of the market and reap the benefits. Also, works that are fictional receive more protection than works that are mostly informative. Generally, facts cannot be copyrighted, although the presentation of them can be.

2. *What is the nature of the use?*

    If the defendant is making a profit from the use, then it is a red flag because they are likely taking money away from the creators who made the work. If a defendant's use is not-for-profit, then it is less likely to be an infringement. Examples of protected use include education, government, politics, news, and other public service organizations. Use in parody or satire is also protected.

3. *What part of the original work was used?*

    There is no set number or percent of a work used; instead, it is the significance of the use. A small sample of a song, just a few seconds, is probably safe if the entire song is five minutes long. But, if the song is only 20 seconds long, then the use is questionable. Also, describing a single scene from a story is probably not a substantial use. But giving away the surprise ending may be if it is the heart of the story. If it is just an incidental use, then it will be protected.

4. *What was the effect on the market for the copyrighted work?*

If the use severely hampers the market for the original work, then it is not a fair use. Once again, the principle is that the creator does not get to reap the benefits of his or her work. (U.S. Copyright Office, n.d.).

As earlier noted, copyright holders have the right to prepare derivatives of their ideas. But if someone were to take copyright work and change it so that it becomes a new creation, then it is not an infringement. This is called a **transformative use or artistically relevant** use and is protected. But the use has to add something to the original work. Courts do not see sampling as a transformative use because it simply takes already recorded music and plays it on a loop.

Parody is considered an artistically relevant use. As previously indicated, fair comment and criticism of a copyrighted work is protected under the Copyright Act. A parody is a commentary that borrows heavily from the original work. But the U.S. Supreme Court has stated that, by definition, a parody has to reference the original work in order to make it commentary (*Campbell v. Acuff-Rose Music, Inc.*, 1994).

Beyond Copyright: Moral Rights in Creative Works

Many jurisdictions outside the United States recognize a "moral right" for authors. Moral rights give additional protection against any use that would be "prejudicial to the author's honor or reputation." The idea is that authors should be able to control the fate of their works and it reputation, not just its monetary value. This would include any unwanted alteration of the work, whether it was positive or negative. For example, making reproduction of a statue or painting may offend the author who worked who believes the value is in the original tangible work. Moral right jurisdictions also require any use of a work, whole or in part, must give attribution to the original author.

Moral rights see creative works as an extension of the author's identity. Thus, an unauthorized use could hurt the integrity of the author. The moral rights are exclusive to the copyright, and authors can retain them even if they give up their copyright. The Berne Convention of 1928, which established international copyright law, includes protections for moral rights.

The United States signed onto the Berne Convention in 1989, but did not adopt its vast protections of moral rights outside of visual art. But the integrity of the work may be protected through other laws such as libel, false advertising and derivative use.

See U.S. Copyright Office (2019). *Authors, attribution, and integrity: Examining moral rights in the United States.*

Protecting One's Identity

Laws protecting one's reputation have been around for close to a millennium. Similarly, there have long been laws against stealing another person's identity, especially when others profit from it. Today, identity theft is a major concern as online data sharing has allowed for personal information to be easily collected and traded (Sciliano, 2019).

Protection of one's image did not develop until the creation of photography. In the early years of the technology, there was a fear of photography. Some people even believed that it was a literal reproduction of their image (Library of Congress, n.d.). It was also at this time that celebrity culture developed. As works of art spread, so could the pictures of the artists who produced them. In the early 1900s, states began to develop laws that protected a person against unwanted public exposure of their likeness (Mulrooney, 2012). Currently, in the United States, 17 states have **misappropriation of likeness** statutes, and another 11 states recognize the common law tort (Digital Media Law Project, n.d.b). There are also protections for celebrities' right to publicity at the federal level through the Lanham Act (Mtima, 2012).

These personality rights are broken into two areas. Generally, misappropriation is the use of someone's name or likeness for commercial purposes without consent (American Law Institute, 1977, Sec. 652). Initially, misappropriation law dealt with plaintiffs who were private persons. In these cases, the plaintiffs had to show that they suffered emotional distress (American Law Institute, 1977). For example, if a company used a photo of you in a billboard advertisement for condoms, and it made it seem like you were inflicted with an STD, then you may be able to sue the company for misappropriation. It is reasonable to believe that a jury would find such a situation to cause emotional distress.

Later, with the rise of celebrity culture, the **right of publicity** came about. These laws deal with public persons who have their likenesses misappropriated. In these cases, the plaintiffs must show an economic injury (American Law Institute, 1977, Sec. 652). If a soft drink firm were to use a picture of Steph Curry or Scarlett Johansson in its commercials without the celebrities' permission, then the company could be sued. The celebrities should have been compensated because the soda company would have profited off the goodwill that the celebrities would have built with the public. Since the right to publicity is an economic or property right, it can be descended to heirs. In the United States, the length of protection after death varies from 25 to 100 years, depending on the state (Digital Media Project, n.d.a).

The name that is used matters, because some names will have value. For example, the name Stefani Germanotta does not have much value in an advertisement, but her stage name, Lady Gaga, does. Moreover, a likeness does not have to be a picture or a name—physical attributes, such as a voice or accent, can be considered a likeness. It can also be the totality of facts. For example, EA Sports, a sports video game publisher, did not have permission from athletes to use their likeness in its college football games. But EA Sports did not use names or likeness. Instead the athletes were described by the team they played on, their positions, uniform numbers, height, weight, and so forth. This was enough information for those who played EA Sports games to identify whom the avatar represented (*Hart v. Electronic Arts, Inc.*, 2013).

Courts have been quite expansive in their interpretation of what is considered likeness, allowing an actor to sue when the character he played was used (*Wendt v. Host International, Inc.*, 1977) and allowing a celebrity to sue when a commercial used a robot dressed similarly to her (*White v. Samsung Electronics*, 1992). Because the right of publicity is an economic right, First Amendment issues are less implicated.

To be misappropriation, the use has to be commercial in nature. Thus, use is always considered commercial in advertisements. But entertainment texts, such as television, games, movies, and so forth, are not considered to be commercial purposes, even though they make a profit (*Sarver v. Chartier*, 2016). Moreover, celebrity names and likenesses can be used in news, including advertising for news programs (e.g., "Tonight on EXTRA! Are Beyonce and Jay Z splitting up?").

However, both entertainment and news can be in violation of right to publicity if the use of the celebrity is the core of the product. For example, in the EA Sports case, without the players, the gamers would likely not buy the product. Thus, the players' likeness was being used for profit (Wiedey, 2018). Also, celebrity impersonators are in violation of right to publicity when they perform the songs, dress like the artists, dance like them, and so forth. Simply doing impressions is not a violation, but performing songs will implicate copyright laws (Boyle, 2012).

News programs can also violate right to publicity. In *Zachini v. Scripps Howard* (1977), the local news station aired the entirety of Hugo Zachini's human cannonball act. He sued for right to publicity. The local news station argued that the broadcast was factual information. The U.S. Supreme Court decided in favor of the human cannonball, stating that by airing the entirety of his act the news station took away his ability to make money off of it. People would watch it for free rather than paying to see him.

The defenses to misappropriation are the same as copyright defenses mentioned previously. If the defendant had received consent to use the plaintiff's likeness, then it is not misappropriation (see Chapter 5). If the defendant's use of a likeness is transformative, then it will be protected (*Campbell v. Acuff-Rose Music, Inc,* 1994). For example, parodies, such as *SNL*, are transformative because they do more than profit off the celebrity image. Finally, if the use is incidental, then it will be protected. If a restaurant were filming a commercial and you happen to walk by in the background, it would be difficult for you to sue if your passing by were incidental. However, if the use of your likeness were integral to the commercial, like in the EA Sports games, then there may be a case (*Hart v. Electronic Arts, Inc.,* 2013).

Virtual Issues in Intellectual Property and Identity Rights

1. **Who will own the troves of data about users that companies collect through connected devices?**

Connected devices collect an almost unlimited amount of data. The data consist of information about the users and their behavior, wants, likes, movement, purchases, and so forth. As users of connected devices, we agree to have this data collected in the terms of service. We also agree to allow the companies to use this data and sell the data for profit. In Chapter 5, we discussed the privacy issues in data collection. But another issue is: Who owns and controls this data?

Data are neither real property nor personal property because they are intangible. Thus, the best bet for a legal protection would be intellectual property law. But data are not an invention or creative. Thus, the person from whom the information is extracted has no property right over it (Determann, 2018). In fact, the companies that created the technology to collect and collate the data have more IP protection because of the originality in their efforts (Determann).

The information these companies collect constructs an identity of you. Facebook knows who you are by looking at your usage. You have also given it permission to use this information to advertise back to you. Social media could also use pictures of you with brand name products to advertise those products to your friends (Cook, 2019). Netflix can use your account activity combined with others in your "taste community" to make suggestions back to you and them (Ernsburger, 2018). Thus, these companies are using your identity to gain good faith with your friends. Word of mouth has always been the most effective advertising, but in the digital context, we are often not as aware of it (Cook, 2019).

One approach to such data use is to provide a right of **data portability**. It would allow people to take the data a company has collected about them, if they choose to sever ties with that company. For example, if you cancelled your Instagram account, Facebook would have to give you all your data back. At a minimum, data portability would allow you to know what data companies have collected on you (Gebhart et al., 2018). Data portability is part of the EU's General Data Protection Regulations, but is not currently recognized in the United States.

2. Do connected devices take away our ownership of the products we buy?

Connected devices allow us to bypass tangible products and own digital copies of everything. We own less hard copy media such as books, magazines, Blu-Ray discs, and CDs. Video games are also now more reliant on streaming. This means fewer products taking up less space in our real world. However, the shift to digital copies has taken away a part of our ownership rights. When we purchase a hard copy, we own the hard copy. We do not have a right to the information produced—the copyright is with the author. But we have the right to do whatever we want with the book, CD, or Blu-Ray disc. We can sell it, rent it, or give it away. We can make a copy or two if we wish (we could not sell hundreds of copies). This is called the **first sale doctrine** (Limitations on Exclusive Rights, 2011).

But when we retrieve content via connected devices, we do not own a copy. With streaming and cloud storage, we have access only to a copy. We have no right to copy, rent, sell, or give it away. In some cases, we can download a copy to our device for instant access. But, most often, the technology does not allow for copies to be made or shared, or it is limited to a number or owned devices. Thus, we no longer purchase copies, we simply license a use (Perzanowski & Schultz, 2018).

But the licensing approach to sales has moved beyond entertainment products. As more devices become smart—appliances, cars, toys—they will have software protected by IP law. These devices will be collecting data on how we eat, sleep, and move. However, consumers who bought these devices will not be able to modify them without running afoul of IP law. If the device is connected, the manufacturers might be able to shut down the device for such an infringement (Walsh, 2014). In many ways, devices that are connected to their original manufacturers take away a property right and replaced it with an access right (Weins, 2015). Along with that, we lose a right to our own information.

3. **Who will own and control the creations that users produce in virtual worlds?**

Virtual worlds are developed by coders. Unlike traditional gaming, many virtual worlds invite users to create and add to the worlds. The software allows entirely new and original worlds to be built. As virtual reality improves, it will also enable users to replicate the real world as well as make creative changes. It is difficult to find anything truly original because it has been often said—all creations are derivative. Whether it is original, a copy, or a derivative, copyright issues will abound.

Original creations in virtual worlds should be protected because the platform is a fixed medium. But a few issues will need to be addressed. What will be considered original? If a user is on an open gaming platform and uses the tools provided by the software developer to create content, who is the actual owner? In analog tech, it is obvious that the photographer is the artist, not the company that makes the camera. The camera developer did not make an artistic creation. In an open gaming setting, if the user creates a virtual property, the extent to which the process was creative must be examined. If the software provides drop menus from which the user chooses, did the user create the property or simply collate the creative possibilities developed by the software company (Caramore, 2008).

As with current gaming, much of this will be governed by the **End User License Agreement (EULA)**. The agreement is the contract between the software developer and the user that provides the terms and conditions of use. As consumers, we are quite familiar with the terms and conditions requirement. We must check a box that said we read them to be able to use the software. However, the reality is that most people do not read the terms because they are long and filled with legal jargon (Cakebread, 2017). Yet, most EULAs spell out the IP rights provided. For example, social media terms and conditions give companies a universal license to use whatever is posted (Nield, 2017). Although the companies do not technically own the copyright, you have agreed to allow them to use your post or virtual creation however they wish because you agreed to the terms and services.

VR software will likely have similar EULAs (as the companies will either be the same tech companies or adopt the industry protocol). The companies will require a universal license to property for users to access the software. These companies also may seek to retain copyright over all property created, arguing that the tools provided by the software were the creative aspect of the creation.

Currently, gaming is quite open to sharing IP and making open source software available (Wallace, 2014). This enables **modders** to change the game at the code level, thereby modifying the software and creating new works. Once again, the EULA will have to govern. Software companies can provide the open source on the condition that they retain the copyright over creations. This is akin to a contracted employee not owning property created in a work place. This may seem unfair, but often is welcomed by gamers who get a chance to change games and be a part of the production.

Since the gaming industry is open to permitting users to create and change software, it is inevitable that users will be inspired by the real world. Thus, they will attempt to insert protected copyrights into the virtual world. Software developers are inspired by the real world, but as businesses they are usually aware of IP law and seek out clearances (or partnerships) to use protected copyrights. One of the most expensive parts of developing games is paying for the licensing rights to brands likes Marvel and Star Wars ("Why Video," 2014).

But when modders create a virtual property that embraces real world copyright and trademarks, it is much more difficult to govern. For example, YouTube had issues with users violating copyright law. Under the DMCA, YouTube was held responsible for copyright infringement if it did not remove the protected works (*Viacom International, Inc. v. YouTube, Inc.*, 2012). Eventually, YouTube decided to pay for license fees to use popular music, but not for movie/television rights (Plaugic, 2017). However, for individual game developers it would not be financially prudent to pay such exorbitant royalties. Moreover, the IP uses may be so individualistic that current licenses would not cover it.

YouTube and other social media users have other defenses such as parody and fair comment. But in a gaming context, this defense is less accepted. Using a Marvel superhero as your avatar is not a parody. In many ways, it is like fan fiction, which is consumers' homage to the franchise they love. But fan fiction is derivative and a copyright infringement (Becker, 2014). Thus, copyright owners must decide if they want to stop such use.

4. Will AI be considered capable of generating originality in copyright law?

Simple AI algorithms are everywhere in our lives. In many ways, they are deciding our artistic preferences. When Netflix and Amazon suggest films to watch or items to purchase, they are basing their recommendations on an analysis of the data we have provided. Some critics argue that this has destroyed the serendipity of being a fan of the arts. When the algorithm feeds only suggestions that are similar to what we—and people assumed to be like us—have already consumed, then they take away some of the free will of humanity (Allnut, 2011). Of course, algorithms cannot appreciate art. AI is simply a function of inputs; thus, a machine cannot create. Creativity is viewed as a purely humanistic endeavor.

But these days, machines are already creating—stories, art, music, and so forth (Elgammel, 2019). When there is a creation, especially when it has economic value, there is a fight over who owns the creation. For AI, the simplest answer is whoever owns the rights to the AI owns the rights to the works. This would follow a similar principle for other works for hire. The animators at PIXAR do not own *Toy Story*, even if they designed the characters. They are contracted to PIXAR (owned by Disney); thus, the corporation owns the copyright.

PIXAR employees sign the contract under their own free will (although it is probably not a totally balanced negotiating relationship). The animators agree to it to be part of the company and allow their work to become part of public viewing. But does the AI have the same rights?

If the AI were designed for the purpose of creating new works and the design were instrumental to new artistic creations, then the designer would have a strong claim. But what if the design simply allowed the AI to learn to create with no more guidance than that. Then through machine learning, it was able to create new works. The AI would more than likely create by copying others. It could study all the classic painters from Renaissance to Postmodern art and then make an amalgam. Copyright requires originality—copies are not protected. But in this case, the AI would not be copying; it would be more akin to a human artist being inspired to create a new work. Ultimately, this process would be no different than other artists who are inspired by those who came before them. Thus, the new work should be protected by copyright.

AI as authors would certainly bring into question of what is truly creative. Ironically, the best way to answer this question may be through the use of AI to judge whether a use of a work violates copyright law. Today, copyright infringement is a question for a judge or jury to decide by considering the testimony of experts in the type of art. For example, basic copyright infringement in music is copied lyrics, beats, hooks, and so forth. In storytelling, it is copied characters, plotlines, scenes, quotes, and so forth. But it is usually pretty clear, with the question being about percentage of use and other defenses such as parody.

The second question is would an audience be confused and believe the two works are the same. For this, it is a question of fact for the jury to consider. In the "Blurred Lines" case, the court found that artists Robin Thicke and Pharrell violated the copyright of Marvin Gaye (owned by his estate) because their new song was too close to the original "essence" of Gaye's song. This widely expands the concept of copyright infringement. With the essence of a work in consideration, what a judge and jury consider to be infringement becomes even more subjective.

Soon, AI could be used instead to make this judgment. It could easily compare the two works and determine an exact percentage of similarity. But it may also be asked to make judgments about whether people would be confused by the similarities. Apps like Spotalike, Same That Tune, and More Tracks Like This provide users with playlists based on the musical attributes of songs the users already like . Similarly, AI could be applied in a copyright case. With essence being a factor, then the pool of comparable songs would expand considerably, but AI could tell a court which works are too similar (Titlow, 2016).

CASE STUDY
My Avatar, My Image, My Property

The Nintendo Wii introduced characters called Miis, which were avatars meant to represent the actual players. This representation did not have to be literal because the system gave users many choices on hair, facial features, skin color, and so forth. If people wanted to get closer to their own image, they could take a picture of themselves and have the system create a Mii from the image. The Mii could be shared with other connected Wii systems and end up in other players' games not connected to the original creator's system. This meant the user's Mii was now out in the world (Irwin, 2017).

The early Miis were very cartoonish. But now, technology allows the creation of more realistic avatars. Like with the Wii system, a player can upload a photo, but the avatar that is created is now close to a realistic portrayal of the user. A player can use that avatar in games and may even be able share it with the world through online connections.

The representation of likeness is not limited to a virtual world. Bots have taken on the identity of people online. Holograms of deceased celebrities, such as Michael Jackson and Tupac Shakur, have appeared in concert with many other celebrity holograms in the works (Tiffany, 2018). It is also not hard to imagine AI being programmed with the identity of a real person. For some people having their memories inserted into an automaton might fulfill a dream of staying alive forever. But what if this avatar, hologram, or robot that resembles you was not created with your permission or your knowledge?

Avatars can be created from any picture. Someone could go to your social media page and take your photos to create an avatar in a virtual world. One day your photos could be used to create a 3-D hologram. Eventually, pictures and videos could be used to create an automaton that represents you. The issue is that these pictures and videos could be taken from online without your permission and then used to develop a new creation of you. A version of you could live in perpetuity in a virtual world that you do not even know exists.

Discussion Questions

1. Who owns the avatar? Does the creator or the company have an intellectual property right in it?

2. If you create an avatar that looks like you, should you have a property right because it is your identity?

3. If someone else creates the avatar that looks like you, should they have an IP right, or should you have a property right to that identity?

4. What if you create a fantasy version of yourself (as a zombie, a fairy, a professional basketball player, and so forth), should it have a property right in your enhanced identity?

5. If you share an avatar that you created, should you be able to stop someone from using it in ways you do not approve (e.g., in virtual worlds or acts)?

CHAPTER 9

Consumer Protection and Market Regulation

I n the 1990s, IBM developed Deep Blue, a computer that would be able to compete against human players in chess. Not only did the computer compete, but it beat renowned chess master Garry Kasparov (Anderson, 2017). It was an impressive feat because, as we all know, chess is a complex game that is difficult to master. Nonetheless, at its core, chess is a game of logic that requires a player to guess the moves of its opponent. In some ways, this is easy for artificial intelligence to process because it can calculate all the possible moves and best probabilities. But could machines beat humans at games with more social context?

Three researchers from Aristotle University in Greece decided to test AI's ability at the board game Monopoly, a game that can involve chance and risk taking. The AI was pitted against two players, one who made consistent rational decisions (e.g., bought only when the player had more than $350) and another player who made decision randomly. In more than 1,000 games, the AI won 70% of the time because it was able to change its strategy depending on which of the two opponents was moving ahead. The researchers concluded that the AI "demonstrated several times an intelligent behaviour of sacrificing some of his temporary wealth in order to invest and secure a more prosperous future" (Bailis et al., 2014, p. 3).

Monopoly is a game that exercises the basic tenets of economics at very low stakes. However, these same principles can be applied on a more significant scale. For example, AI could be used to analyze markets to find inefficiencies and promote competition, or it could be used to manipulate markets and control the world economy. Nations have **antitrust laws** in place that outlaw price fixing and collusion. Yet, using algorithms to determine pricing has become more standard in commerce. Currently, Amazon implements over two million price changes each day using its algorithms as it reacts to people's purchases (Himes & Song, 2019). Uber and Lyft use the same variables in their algorithms to determine prices, but have no stated agreement between the competitors (Himes & Song). As more industries adopt the practice of algorithmic pricing, will it be considered unlawful collusion or an innovative approach to business?

This chapter examines how advancement in technology can affect consumer markets and corporate power. First, it reviews contemporary law regulating corporations and protecting consumers. Second, it discusses looming issues in emerging media and potential changes in antitrust and consumer protections law.

Legal Principles in Market Regulation

Today, most Americans are concerned with the current power of corporations and the lack of government regulation (Rifken, 2016). But this concern is not new. Since the 19th century, corporations have played a significant role in the everyday lives of Americans. But over the last 50 years, changes in technology and regulation have allowed a renewed concentration of wealth and power. Currently, the revenue of the Fortune 500 companies makes up 74% of the U.S. GDP, and the Fortune 100 companies comprise 46% (Flowers, 2015). Moreover, recent legal decisions have seemed to give corporations more rights than they have ever had.

Although the idea of a corporation being a legal person is still a political controversy, it is actually well established in U.S. law (Center for American Progress, 2012). Since mercantile corporations began in the 17th century, they have sought the protections of contracts, property, and liability laws. In the early 1800s, the U.S. Supreme Court stated that corporations have the same legal rights as real persons to own property and make contracts (*Society for the Propagation of the Gospel in Foreign Parts v. The Town of New Haven*, 1823). In 1868, the Court expanded the scope of the 14th Amendment to include corporations, providing equal protection in commercial and tax law. Although the official opinion does not state that corporations are legal persons, it was adopted by other courts as precedent (*San Mateo v. Southern Pacific Railroad*, 1885).

By the end of the 20th century, the U.S. Supreme Court had extended civil liberties to corporations. In the 1970s, the Court granted corporations freedom of speech (*First National Bank of Boston v. Bellotti*, 1978). About 40 years later, the Court stated that because money is speech, the government could not put a limit on the amount of money that corporations spend on political speech, although there are caps on direct donations to candidates (*Citizens United v. Federal Election Commission*, 2010). The Court then extended civil rights of corporations to include a limited right to the free exercise of religion (*Sebelius v. Hobby Lobby*, 2013). However, critics fear that, as legal persons, corporate civil liberties might continue to expand to include other rights such as the right to own weapons and the right to vote (Clifford, 2010). This would give corporations even more power in our everyday lives.

Corporate Speech: Commercial to Political

Commercial speech, is public communication used during business, such as in advertising and marketing. For most of our legal history, it did not receive free speech protection.. Courts considered commercial speech to be of lesser value because it was paid for and consisted of verifiable statements. In addition, there was a history of abuse and fraud in advertising. But, in the 1970s, the U.S. Supreme Court officially recognized that commercial speech had value to consumers and deserved some protection (*Virginia State Pharmacy Board v. Virginia Citizens Consumer Council*, 1976). However, the government can still regulate false advertising and truthful advertising.

FALSE ADVERTISING

False advertising can always be regulated and punished. This includes false endorsements, lies, distortion, and withholding facts. For example, in 2016, the FTC filed a suit against Volkswagen for making claims that its diesel engines burned clean fuel, when in fact, VW had created software that allowed its cars to emit cleaner exhaust when being tested (Federal Trade Commission, 2016).

When determining whether an advertisement is false, regulatory agencies use a **reasonable consumer** standard (Federal Trade Commission, 2015). Claims such as a restaurant having the "world's best coffee" may not be true. Such **puffery** is allowed because a reasonable consumer knows it is not a literal claim. But companies often walk a fine line when it comes to puffery and false advertising. For example, in advertisements for restaurants, food staging is often used to make food look better. Then consumers are often disappointed when the food they get from the restaurant does not look like the food from the advertisement.

Factual claims made in marketing and advertising must be true. This includes key words used, many of which are defined by either government or industry standards. For example, the FDA regulates many claims such as the definition of low-fat or low calories. To have these labels, a product must meet certain nutritional standards (e.g., low fat is less than 3 g of fat per serving)

(Nutrient Content Claims, 2012). But other claims such as "artisanal" are not regulated (Bell, 2013).

Once a word is used long enough by an industry, then regulating agencies usually will make a rule to define it. For example, if a package claims to be "light," it has to meet certain nutritional measures. Companies tried to skirt this by using the term "lite" instead of "light." However, the FDA eventually caught on and made the same requirements for the two terms (Nutrient Content Claims, 2012).

TRUTHFUL ADVERTISING

The U.S. Supreme Court developed a legal test to determine when the government can regulate truthful advertising (*Central Hudson Gas & Electric Corp. v. Public Service Commission*, 1980). It can regulate truthful advertising if:

1. The state has a substantial interest (e.g., health, safety, fairness);
2. The regulation directly advances interest; and
3. The interest and the regulation are rationally related.

When it comes to regulating commercial speech, the government usually has a substantial interest in protecting the health and safety of the consumers who buy the products, especially those that are inherently dangerous such as alcohol, cigarettes, and pharmaceuticals. But courts have found that advertising regulation is often overbroad in its regulation of speech. Since the commercial speech test was developed in 1980, the U.S. Supreme Court has slowly limited the ability of the government to regulate advertising. For example, a Massachusetts law required that tobacco advertisements in stores be placed above 5 feet to fight underage smoking. The Court struck it down as overly broad, stating: "Not all children are less than 5 feet tall, and those who are can look up and take in their surroundings" (*Lorillard v. Reilly*, 2001). The Court has also hinted that any regulation of truthful advertising may be suspect because it would regulate commercial speech based on its message, and content-based regulations are unconstitutional (*Sorrell v. IMS Health Inc.*, 2011). When Rhode Island banned the advertising of alcohol prices to promote temperance, the Court stated that the solution to serving the state's interest is not to bar the advertiser's speech. Instead, the government should start public service campaigns in favor of temperance (*Liquormart, Inc. v. Rhode Island*, 1996).

Finally, the line between whether corporate speech is commercial or is political is blurring. The distinction is critical because commercial speech still receives less protection, whereas political speech receives almost absolute protection. But more and more corporate speech is both commercial and political. For example, when Nike airs a commercial with Colin Kaepernick in its "Believe in Something" campaign, it is a shoe company that is building goodwill with many consumers. But it is also purposely making a political statement (Santos, 2018).

Are Regulations on Advertising Unconstitutional?

Throughout the 20th century, the U.S. Supreme Court stated that advertising was not a form of protected speech due in part to the history of lies and distortion. But, in the 1970s, the U.S. Supreme Court granted free speech protection to commercial speech. The legal test was intermediate scrutiny, which was less protection than political speech. It still required the government to show an important interest in regulating advertising and that the regulation substantially served the reason behind it. For example, pharmaceutical advertisements must list their products' side effects so that consumers will be informed about them before they ask their doctor about the products.

But in the last 30 years, the U.S. Supreme Court has seen few commercial speech regulations that it has liked. In case after case, the Court has found that the government went too far in its regulations. For example, in *IMS v. Sorrell* (2014), the Court examined a Vermont state law that barred insurance companies from selling identifiable health data to pharmaceutical companies, which would use the data to market products. The state argued that it was a regulation of commercial activity meant to protect the professional standards of doctors and the doctor-patient relationship. Pharmaceutical companies challenged the law as a violation of free speech.

The U.S. Supreme Court overturned the law, holding that it was aimed at the speaker and the message, which is almost always unconstitutional. Then, in *NIFLA v. Becarra* (2018), the U.S. Supreme Court held that a California law that required licensed "prolife" centers to provide clients information about the availability of state-funded abortions was suspect. The Court stated that the law likely violates the First Amendment because it is a content-based regulation that compels the centers to speak a certain message they do not want to speak. The Court recognized that professionals may be compelled to "disclose factual, noncontroversial information in their commercial speech" as long as it only "incidentally burden[s] speech."

These cases, along with *Citizens United v. Federal Election Commission* (2010), which extends the free speech rights of corporations, suggest that the precedent of treating advertising speech differently than other forms of protected speech is in jeopardy. Inherently, any commercial speech regulation is aimed at a particular speaker—a business—and so can be considered unconstitutional content-based regulation. Many commercial speech regulations require businesses to reveal information such as ingredients, prices, side effects, and so forth, which could be considered unconstitutionally compelled speech. As the U.S. Supreme Court grants more protections for corporations, it is likely that lower forms of scrutiny for commercial speech will soon come to an end.

See Calvert, C. (2019). Is everything a full-blown first amendment case after Becerra and Janus? Sorting out standards of scrutiny and untangling "speech as speech" cases from disputes incidentally affecting expression. *Michigan State Law Review*, 73–132. https://digitalcommons.law.msu.edu/lr/vol2019/iss1/3

Government Regulation

In the 19th century, print media did not have special regulation beyond the laws applied to all speech, such as obscenity, libel, and copyright (*Miami Herald Publishing Co. v. Tornillo*, 1974; *Red Lion Broadcasting Co. v. Federal Communications Commission*, 1969). But when electronic communication appeared in the late 1800s, the government took an active role in regulating the structure and activity of the industries.

One reason was that electronic media needed a massive infrastructure. Telegraph and later telephone required the laying of cables across the country. It had to be regulated because the physical restrictions made it so that only one set of lines could be installed. Moreover, the government saw communications as a **public good** that everyone in the nation needed (Bonnett, 2001). So, the government invested in its growth in order to give everyone access. As with other public goods (e.g., railroad, electricity, water), the government either directly provides the service or gives a company a monopoly over the industry in exchange for fixed, low prices and almost universal access.

In the early part of 20th century, the federal government decided to regulate broadcasting and treat it as a public good. The Radio Act of 1927 declared that the airwaves belonged to the public, and frequencies would be licensed out. In exchange, the licensee would have to serve the **"public interest, convenience and necessity."** (Radio Act, 1927). Over the years, licensees have had to meet the public interest requirement by airing public affairs and children's programming, giving political candidates access, and so forth. They also were prohibited from broadcasting indecency (Radio Act, 1927). In 1949, the government implemented the **Fairness Doctrine**, which required broadcasters to air both sides of any political issue or give the other side a chance to reply (*Red Lion Broadcasting Co. v. FCC*, 1969). But after the 1970s, the rules were not enforced, and they were repealed in 1987 as the government deregulated telecommunications (Boliek, 2011). Recently, concerns about political bias of social media companies has prompted discussions about bringing the Fairness Doctrine back (Almond, 2018).

The Communications Act of 1934 placed the Federal Communications Commission (FCC) in charge of overseeing the telecommunications industry. The FCC has broad powers to regulate the industry including making rules, enforcing rules, and adjudicating hearings. Licensees can get a judicial review of FCC decisions. Courts will consider if the agency's decision is **"arbitrary and capricious."** (*Federal Communications Commission v. Fox Television Stations, Inc.*, 2012). This low standard of review gives great deference to the regulatory agency—as long as the agency has a reason for its decision, then it will stand.

Net Neutrality: On and Off Again?

Net Neutrality is the principle that internet service providers (ISPs) will treat all data the same. They will not slow down or speed up certain sites. They also will not charge customers different rates for the different types of sites they use.

In the early days of the internet, the FCC decided that the internet was not a public good. Thus, it was be regulated like content providers, and ISPs were free to charge different rates. Over the next decade there were attempts to pass a net neutrality rule. The cable and phone industry, the primary ISPs in the United States, argued against such a rule. They claimed it would allow a free ride for the content companies such as Netflix, Google, and Facebook that garnered much of the traffic but did not pay for infrastructure. Proponents of net neutrality argued that the policy would destroy the essence of the internet, which was always for start-ups and innovators. Moreover, the ISPs would control the content and give preferences to their own. There was evidence that ISPs had throttled some services while advantaging others (Karr, 2018).

During the Obama Administration, the FCC passed net neutrality laws, which were eventually challenged by the ISPs. Courts ruled that net neutrality rules could stand only if the FCC changed the status of ISPs from information services to **common carriers**. In 2015, the FCC did this, and the net neutrality rules were put in place. However, under the Trump Administration, the rules were repealed. Ultimately, Congress could pass a net neutrality law making it more permanent but has not done so yet.

Antitrust and Competition Law

The end of the 19th century is often referred to as the Gilded Age. It was the era of the robber barons—the captains of industry such as Carnegie, Rockefeller, and Vanderbilt who controlled large amounts of wealth through their monopolies. The concern was that the concentration in power would hurt consumers because the monopolies would not have to compete, which would lead to higher prices. Also, with no competition, the monopolies would have no incentive to innovate. The concerns also moved beyond economic. Critics believed that the concentration in power threatened democracy through political corruption and bribery (Stucke & Grunes, 2001).

In response to the concerns, the U.S. government passed the Sherman Antitrust Act (1890) in order to protect consumer welfare (*Brown Shoe Co. v. United States*, 1962; Paquette, 2017). It allows both criminal punishment as well as civil cases against corporations. Section 1 of the act focuses on collusion by two or more companies in an industry. Section 2 deals with attempts to monopolize an industry. **Antitrust** cases can be brought by the government, competitors, or consumers, and awards can be tripled (thus a jury award of $1 million could pay out $3 million). Many states also have their own separate antitrust laws (Eisenach & Kulik, 2019).

The U.S. Supreme Court has read section 2 of the Sherman Act to require: "(1) that a firm possess monopoly power and (2) that it intentionally behaves in such a way as to obtain, maintain, or expand such power" (*United States v. Grinnell Corporation*, 1966, pp. 570–571). Thus, a company has to behave in a way that artificially creates a monopoly. **Natural monopolies** are usually allowed because they simply outperform everyone else by offering a better product. The U.S. Supreme Court has stated that it would be counterproductive to the consumer to bar such innovation (*Copperweld Corp. v. Independence Tube Corporation*, 1984).

When determining whether a firm is a monopoly, courts do not need to have a finding of 100% control. Instead, courts look at a firm's ability to control prices or supply in the market (*United States v. E. I. du Pont de Nemours & Co.*, 1956). In some cases, the actual market share is indeterminate as a low market share can result in high market power or vice versa. The main concern is how the company's activity impacts consumers.

An example of illegal company activity is **price fixing**. This can occur when several companies in an industry form an explicit cartel and agree to set high prices. Without an explicit agreement, price fixing is difficult to prove (Federal Trade Commission, 2019). **Parallel pricing**, in which companies monitor competitors and follow suit, is legal. Another form of illegal price fixing is **predatory pricing**, when one powerful company sets prices extremely low and takes a loss until all its competitors go out of business. Forced bundling can also be illegal. In the 1990s, the federal government sued Microsoft for its bundling of the Internet Explorer browser system with its Windows operating system, thereby hindering the ability of third-party browsers to be used with Windows (*United States v. Microsoft Corporation*, 2001). The case was settled out of court.

When it comes to the Department of Justice enforcing antitrust law against the media industries, the rules are different. Media companies sell information, which is critical to a functioning democracy. If a cosmetics or shoe company becomes a monopoly, it could hurt consumers when it comes to pricing and choice. But it is unlikely that a shoe monopoly will have a profound impact on the nation. However, when media industries are concentrated, it could threaten democracy because dissemination of information would be concentrated (Stucke & Grunes, 2001). For example, in 2018, Sinclair Broadcast Group made 193 of its local U.S. affiliates read the same political editorial on their local news programming (Matthews, 2018). In 2002, when a train carrying chemicals derailed in Minot, North Dakota, the government sent out a warning to be aired on broadcast stations. When the warning system malfunctioned, local authorities called radio stations to relay the message. But, seven of the nine radio stations were syndicated stations and had no one at the stations to take the calls (Shafer, 2007).

Even though media's impact may be greater, enforcing antitrust law in the industry is difficult because it implicates the First Amendment. Media companies often use the First Amendment as a shield against regulation, but courts often use the expansion of the "marketplace of ideas" as justification for regulation (*Turner Broadcasting v. Federal Communications Commission*, 1994). Moreover, when it comes to media mergers, the DOJ often has had difficulty figuring out **market concentration**. With a traditional consumer good, market concentration is determined by examining the number of products sold. For example, for a shoe company, the government would look at the number of total shoes sold in the marketplace and the percent that were from one company (Department of Justice, 2018). The percentage has varied in the past, but today, a few companies can control 75% to 90% of the market before the DOJ will act. As long as there are two or three strong players in the market (often called a duopoly or **oligopoly**), then the government will not act (Wu, 2013).

But with media companies, this equation is much more difficult to calculate. In determining the market, it is unclear what is to be measured—is it traffic, ratings, or content produced? The regulating body also has to figure out the competition. But in media, there is always a question as to the breadth of the market—is it the genre, medium, all media, or all entertainment? When it comes to media concentration, the Department of Justice has mostly defaulted to advertising sales, which the majority of media companies use as a pricing model. If the advertisers have choices among sites that competed, then the market is considered sufficiently competitive (Stucke & Grunes, 2001).

When telecommunication companies (phone, broadcasting, or internet service) seek to merge, they not only have to be approved by the DOJ, but the FCC also has its own rules. In radio broadcasting, companies can own as many stations as they can afford, but there are caps on the numbers in one city (maximum of eight in the largest cities). With television stations, a company's total available viewership cannot surpass 40% of the population (Federal Communications Commission, 2017).

When it comes to other forms of media, the FCC has limited regulatory power unless the service is ancillary to broadcasting or telephone service. Thus, the FCC does not regulate networks, cable, satellite, or streaming content. But it does regulate internet service providers, because they are often cable and phone companies (see Net Neutrality text box) (Federal Communications Commission, n.d.)

Examples of Antitrust Concerns in Media

AT&T [Bell Telephone] (1982): The company had a near monopoly over telephone service in the United States. After an antitrust suit, the company agreed to divest into seven companies. AT&T has since bought back four of the companies. The other two today are CenturyLink and Verizon.

Microsoft (1998): The Department of Justice brought an antitrust case against Microsoft for bundling its Windows operating system with Internet Explorer. The final consent agreement required Microsoft computing interfaces to be compatible with other browsers.

AOL-Time Warner (1999): First major attempt at a merger between digital and traditional content companies, which was ultimately unsuccessful. In reviewing the merger, the government required Time Warner cable distribution to be open to other ISPs.

Comcast/NBC Universal Merger (2011): The first major merger between distributor and content creators, beginning the traditional media companies' attempts to mitigate losses to digital platforms. The government required that for seven years, Comcast charge digital and traditional distributors the same prices.

Time Warner/AT&T (2018): The DOJ unsuccessfully attempted to block a merger between telecomm and content companies because the court said that the merger allowed the companies to compete against big tech. There were no conditions to the merger

Google (the 2010s): Throughout the decade, the U.S. government investigated the practices of the tech giant, but it never filed a suit. Under the Trump administration, the DOJ has continued to probe several big tech companies with calls for bringing an antitrust case gaining momentum.

Virtual Issues in Consumer Protection and Market Regulation

1.   Will advertising be so integrated into virtual reality that consumers will not know they are being marketed to?

Generally, consumers do not like advertising. Since the invention of the remote control, advertisers have been dealing with the issue of how to make sure the consumer actually hears or sees the ads. From television to social media to mobile gaming, consumers are inundated with advertising—of course that does not mean the consumer is engaged. Today, the popularity of ad blockers and subscription services like Netflix illustrates the public's disdain for advertising. One solution for advertisers is to place ads in the content, including product placement, company sponsorship, and **native advertising,** which is advertising designed to look like content. Of course, there is a calculus as to how much advertising consumers will tolerate (Lovasz, 2017).

VR screens show traditional ads, such as logos, banners, and short videos. But, again, there is a limit to how many can be displayed before they destroy the immersive experience. Additionally, using connected devices with VR or haptic technology, companies could track **biometrics** such as eye gaze, pupil dilation, heart rate, sweat, and so forth (Harrell, 2019). AI on social media already makes decisions about which ads to show based on user information collected. But more advanced tech will allow more information and better judgement. Advertising placement in VR technology could move beyond which ads you prefer, to which advertisements create excitement, because the marketers could read your subtle physiological responses. At that point, ads know you better than you know yourself.

Free mobile games are filled with ads, while other games, called **advergames**, integrate products into the game itself (Sharma, 2014). Virtual worlds like *Minecraft* and *Roblox* also incorporate product placement into games. Having avatars use real life products makes the virtual world seem more real. The avatar could drink a Coke, drive a Jaguar, or eat at Sonic Drive-In. It is also an opportunity for companies to buy virtual space. VR designers could give lots of product choices to players in the game and sell the advertising "space" to companies (Harwell, 2016). They also could give exclusive deals similar to those social influencers on social media get. If virtual worlds were to do this, they may have to make disclosures that companies paid for it, as is the case with advertising and blogger endorsements (Federal Trade Commission, 2017).

2. **Will advancements in technology make advertising and marketing more effective, requiring greater regulation?**

For centuries, the goal of advertising has been to create an emotional connection between the consumer and the product. From the earliest days of advertising, marketers used strong emotions like fear and lust to move the consumer. Today, television ads may never mention a product at all; instead, they tell us a story meant to create a feeling. For both, the idea is the same—to transfer the value of the advertisement's message to the product itself.

AR/VR allows companies to enhance this effect because the technology immerses the consumer into the marketing experience. For example, Bareburger's AR campaign on Snapchat enabled customers to view its products from anywhere. The customers could see 3-D images of its products, including the sizzling meat and melted cheeses (Liffreing, 2018). In Adidas's VR campaign, customers could climb mountains with famous athletes. Rather than the celebrity simply saying how great the product is, the customer got to see the company's product in use through a unique VR experience (Bonasio, 2017).

Virtual reality technology has also changed the shopping experience. People can go to stores and get enhanced experiences using the technology. People can also choose to stay home and use VR apps that allow them to have the complete tactile experiences of shopping. Amazon, which has already diverted millions into staying home to shop, now enables people to use VR try-ons. Customers can see how a shoe, a shirt, or wearable tech will look on them (Bonasio, 2017). With Ikea's AR app, people can visualize how furniture will fit and look in their rooms at home (Forsey, 2018). In car sales, customers can experience virtually how a car operates from the steering to the radio to the sounds the engine makes ("Now You Can," 2014).

Of course, all of this requires a level of trust that the virtual is a close replication of the real experience. Companies live off the goodwill they build with consumers. Consumers' complaints and boycotts can be negative for a company (Reed & Samuelson, 2017). Thus, it will be in the companies' best interests to provide the most engaging and accurate experience for shoppers. However, in industries in which the competition is low, companies can be less than truthful and often unhelpful. For decades, Comcast and other cable distributors have rated among the lowest in customer satisfaction. Despite the bad publicity, these companies did not need to change because they had a monopoly in most of their markets (Bode, 2018).

Since many industries are highly concentrated with little competition in the market, consumers may need legal remedies. If a product is dangerous or completely ineffective, then consumers can sue. But many times, if the product is simply poorly made or does not live up to its marketing, there is very little recourse outside of complaining to the wider public if it will listen. Any attempt to sue would not be worth the cost in time and money. Ultimately, it is buyer beware (Ciccone, 2012).

This is often where government and industry regulations fill a void. The FTC may have to make additional rules about VR shopping. If there is fraudulent or false advertising, then the government should be able to fine the company no matter the medium. The government could also require warnings to be displayed in the virtual world as the customer shops, similar to the requirements for television advertisements.. But the warning text on television is often very small and flashes quickly on the screen. The concern is whether this would effectively counter the power of VR. Conversely, the advertisers would want nothing to interfere with the customers' engagement with the immersive environment. With courts granting more protection to commercial speech, corporations may be able to make an argument that such regulations move beyond what is necessary. In addition, courts may adopt a justification that, with more information available to consumers, they should be more able to defend themselves against marketing (Cortez, 2013).

3. **Are tech companies becoming so important and powerful in our lives that they need to be regulated like a public good or even broken up to force competition?**

People spend most of their waking hours with media, nearly 11 hours a day interacting with it in some form (Nielson Research Group, 2018). On average, we spend 2 hours a day on social media, an hour a day gaming, and 4 hours a day watching videos (Anderton, 2019). But the media landscape is vast, with so many options for platforms, genres, programs, artists, and so forth. It would seem market concentration in media would be of little concern. However, if we look at where we spend most of our time during the day, the picture is a little different.

The most popular social media site is Facebook, and users spend 38 minutes a day on the site. The second most popular site is Instagram, which is owned by Facebook. Users are on Instagram about 24 minutes a day. The third most popular social media app is Messenger, also owned by Facebook. Combined, users spend average nearly an hour a day with a Facebook product (Carbone, 2019).

About 96% of all online searches go through Google (Desjardins, 2018). Alphabet, Google's parent company, also owns YouTube. Around the world, people watch 1 billion hours of YouTube videos a year, compared to 1.25 billion hours watching all other television programming (Bergman, 2017).

Netflix has 62 million paid subscribers in the United States, which makes it the largest single television distributor in the country, without counting the multiple accounts per subscriber (Meek, 2019). If you are watching Netflix, you may be watching it via Google, Chromecast, or Apple TV. You may be watching it on your Apple iPhone or Google Chromebook. Or, you could be a brand loyalist and watch television and movies through Amazon Prime on your Amazon Fire Tablet.

These are a few examples of how the big tech companies—Facebook, Amazon, Apple, Google, IBM, and Microsoft (together called the MAFIA-G)—as well as a few Chinese companies (Baidu, Alibaba, Tencen, and Huawei—together called BATH) are taking market share in the media world (Sterling, 2019). Their meteoric rise as distributors of hardware and content has enabled them to invest in making their own content. This has allowed them to compete directly with the traditional content producers, such as Disney, Viacom, and Comcast, which have, in turn, moved into technology to compete with the MAFIA-G in the United States.

But when it comes to emerging tech, the traditional companies have not been able to compete with the financing and expertise of the big tech companies. In VR hardware, Facebook, Samsung, and HTC control 73% of the market, with Samsung controlling 43%. Amazon, Google, and Apple have 75% of the market on virtual assistants, with Apple's Siri controlling 46% (Statista, 2020).

Conversely, when other small companies have any success, the big tech companies quickly buy the competition and further consolidate. The big tech companies are pouncing on start-ups and absorbing their human capital and intellectual property rights (Ciccatelli, 2018). The big tech companies have the resources to further develop the technology and quickly, which they do only when it is to their own advantage. Innovation can be stifled if it does not fit their business plans. Moreover, innovation often comes from collaboration, but consolidation makes this a non-starter (it can be illegal collusion).

More importantly, the significant role that this technology plays in our lives gives significant power to the big tech companies. There is already a concern about how much power these tech companies have and the impact on our lives. In both the United States and the European Union, governments are interrogating the big tech companies and considering whether they are monopolies exerting too much power (Associated Press, 2019). The lack of regulation over the last 30 years has allowed these companies to develop into large conglomerates. Already, big tech's revenue makes them larger than many national economies (Belinchón & Maynihan, 2018). This has enabled great growth in technology and provided many benefits in our lives. But the unforeseen consequences have also impacted consumers, including issues already discussed in this book such as privacy, defamation, hate speech, politics, and so forth.

If left unchecked, the big tech companies' power may become even greater. The information they will be able to collect through connected devices will allow their AI to analyze consumers and competitors alike. They will be able to give consumers exactly what they want and need, for which there is no competition. The amount of information collected and the ability to process it will create an insurmountable **barrier to entry** to the market ("How to Tame," 2018). The tech companies could then legally buy up all start-ups and invest their vast amounts of money into further research and development. Eventually, these industries would become strong legal duopolies split among a handful of international conglomerates.

But, if we consumers get exactly what we want, we may feel little concern because the market is serving us. When customers are happy, there is generally very little regulatory oversight as there is no political will to encourage it. The amount of time, money, and information we dedicate to these services will give them great power to control all aspects of what we do. The amount of information they collect rivals the government surveillance conducted by the most advanced nations. But unlike governments, the companies are not bound by legal limitations regarding surveillance. In fact, for the most part, only they regulate their activities. But it is difficult, because they are using fair business practices. They are natural monopolies, or strong oligopolies, that have outperformed others. They are no different than other industries that have a few companies that control most of the market.

We give up protections of privacy, identity, and property rights when we use these services. We agree to it in the terms of services (which we do not read). But we are satisfied when we get to be an avatar in a virtual world, have an app tell us the best nutrition plan for us, or have a digital assistant waiting for us to speak to it. The trade is seemingly worth it. But if one day we decide it has gone too far, the protections and rights will be difficult to get back.

Nations are considering using antitrust laws to break up or slow down these tech giants. But governments are concerned because our relationship with this technology is different. Antitrust laws would have to be amended based on the industry's impact. In the United States the broadcasting industry was treated differently by having a second level of ownership rules enforced by the FCC. These rules were more stringent because the FCC considered telecommunications to be a public good. Maybe technology will be considered the same, and these companies will be broken up into smaller companies, like Bell Telephone was in the 1980s. However, a better way to open up innovation may be to keep the companies intact, but force them to open up patents, separate hardware from software, and make sure their products are compatible, with options for competitors (Chakravorti, 2019).

CASE STUDY
Your Brain as a Connected Device

In the movie *Ready Player One,* an evil corporation, the internet Research Board, is trying to win control of "The Oasis," a virtual world where almost everyone goes to escape reality. The CEO of the corporation is sure he will win control of the platform, so he is already dreaming of how it can be exploited. In one scene, he explains to the board of directors his plan to monetize the game: "Research shows we can sell 80% of the screen without inducing seizures" (internet Movie Database, n.d.).

The movie may be a glimpse into the future, but we already have seen the explosion of advertising from sports uniforms to cable television screens to social media feeds. There are even billboards on people's private property and sponsored advertisement on people's bodies. If there is space, then it will be sold (Shontell, 2011). It seems that the only space that has not been commodified is inside our minds. But that may change too.

Depictions of the future often show people wearing AR/VR goggles that allow them to receive a personalized online feed they can control with their hands or gaze. But could we move one step further and have a feed in our "mind's eye," without the hardware?

In 2017, researchers in South Africa were able to connect human brain activity to the internet. This is possible because the brain is like any other machine that produces electrical signals, which can be collected and connected to a device. This early research allows the user's brain activity to be uploaded to the internet for research. Brain-computer interfaces (BCI) are already being used to enable persons who are paralyzed to drive wheelchairs (Tang et al., 2018). In the popular press, BCI research, dubbed "Braininternet," has been described as turning the brain "into an internet of Things (IoT) node on the World Wide Web" (Caughill, 2017, para. 1).

Naturally, the next step would be to reverse the process, so that users could "upload" the internet into their brains. A company called Neuralink is attempting to create a chip that could be implanted in the brain (Hasselton, 2018).

The technology is far off, but with it, users could access the internet directly inside their minds. Then the mind's eye would see an internet screen and an augmented reality.

Tech companies have been using research from human psychology to try to keep people addicted to their phones and social media sites (Haubursin, 2017). By offering "free" products, companies have been attempting to keep people constantly attached so that the companies can sell more advertising. Marketing also has moved from the mass markets of television to the microtargeting of mobile so it can be more efficient. These days, we are given carefully curated advertisements and choices about ad preferences.

A direct feed to the mind would be the holy grail for marketers. Rather than marketers reading cookies or big data to ascertain consumers' attitudes, the direct connection could read brain activity to get to the true self. Marketers could place an advertisement on the mind's "screen" with a guarantee that it will be seen. Or, maybe more effective would be to code the advertisement into electrical signals that bypass the visual cortex of the brain (Cohen, 2013). The fear of subliminal messages might finally become a real concern.

Discussion Questions

1. How much of virtual space should be commodified?

2. Should companies be allowed to use "connected brains" for marketing purposes? Why or why not?

3. If so, to what extent, should attempts to commercialize thought be regulated?

4. Should individual consumers and the market be able to self-regulate? Why or why not?

Glossary

Actual Malice A fault standard requiring that the plaintiff show that the defendant either knew the statement was false or had a reckless disregard as to whether it was.

Administrative Rules Laws passed by government agencies (e.g., FCC).

Advergames gamesthat include branded products as part of the content.

All-Purpose Public Figures In defamation law, plaintiffs who are well known and powerful enough to defend themselves. They must prove actual malice.

Alternative Dispute Resolution Solving legal disputes through means other than a court case (e.g., arbitration, negotiation).

Amicus Brief Documents filed in a case by a third party who has an interest in the outcome.

Antitrust Laws Regulates the economic concentration and control of industries. Monopolies are illegal.

Arbitrary and Capricious A legal standard used by courts to judge the reasonableness of executive agency decisions.

Artificial Intelligence Any machine that has been programmed to learn. Today it is software that learns large amounts of information in order to complete a task.

Augmented Reality A hybrid of natural environment and computer-generated environment.

Barriers to Entry Obstacles that make it difficult for new companies to start up in an industry (e.g., technology, labor, costs, etc.).

Beyond a Reasonable Doubt The burden of proof for prosecution of criminal law.

Big Data Large sets of data often collected from online activity and connected devices.

Biometrics Measurements related to human characteristics (e.g., fingerprints, pulse, DNA, etc.).

Black Letter Law Undisputed and long-standing principles of law.

Checks and Balances Structural separation of government powers to ensure that branches are equal

Civil Law Laws enforced by individual parties through lawsuits.

Civil Liability A person is legally responsible for an injury and has to pay damages.

Cloud Computing Storage of data through a private or public network of remote servers.

Commercial Speech Speech used in business, including trademarks, advertising, PR, and marketing.

Common Carriers In information services, the company that own the distribution channels must open its channels for other services.

Common Law Law derived from precedent rather than a statute.

Communication Technology Technological aids used for communication purposes, including phones, radios, televisions, and computers.

Compensatory Damages Jury awards that make up for actual money losses to the plaintiff.

Confidentiality Laws that bar people in certain relationships (e.g., spouse, doctors, employee, etc.) from providing protected information.

Consequential Ethics Using the results of your actions as the guide to deciding what is right or wrong.

Content-Based Regulations Government regulation of speech based on the speaker or the message. These laws are almost always unconstitutional.

Contributory Infringement In copyright law, when a party's action or inaction are partially responsible for a copyright infringement.

Contributory Negligence In negligence law, when a party's actions are partially responsible for the injury.

Cookies Messages from visited websites that are stored on your browser.

Copyright A legal protection for original creations fixed to a medium.

Criminal Incitement When a speaker intentionally calls for others to commit a crime and the audience immediately reacts (e.g., inciting a riot).

Criminal Law Statutes passed to protect the public and enforced by the government.

Cyberlockers Online file sharing services that provide massive data storage for uploaded content.

Dark Web A network of encrypted sites not available through commercial search engines.

Data Portability The ability for people to be able to take the data a company has collected about them, if they choose to sever ties.

Deepfake Video or audio that has been manipulated using AI to replace the original person with someone else.

Defamation A general term for laws against spreading false statement that injure another person's reputation (e.g., libel and slander).

Derivative Use In copyright law, a work based on a previous work.

Designated Public Forum The government decides to open government-owned land to speech. The government can regulate speech by time and manner.

Digital Fingerprint The unique set of data we leave when we use connected devices.

Doxing The publication or threat to expose private (or semi-public) information about you online with malicious intent.

Duty of Care In tort law, when parties have an obligation to use reasonable care over their actions.

Emerging Communication Technology Newer or enhanced forms of communication technology such as connected devices, virtual reality, holograms, robots, that became commercial in the 21st century.

End User License Agreement (EULA) The contract between the developer and the user of the software that provides the terms and conditions of use.

Ethics A set of moral principles that guide our behavior.

Executive Branch Implements or enforces the law (e.g., law enforcement).

Executive Orders Presidential declarations that give direction to federal agencies.

Fairness Doctrine An FCC rule that required broadcasters that discussed a political issue to provide both sides of the issue or give access to the opposing side (Repealed in 1987).

Fair Use In copyright, another party can use a copyrighted work for limited purposes (e.g., news, education, parody, etc.).

False Light A tort law that bars publication of misleading information that is highly offensive. Public figures must prove actual malice in a false light case.

False Pretenses In intrusion cases, a defendant cannot gain access to private places by lying.

Falsity In defamation law, a public figure plaintiff must prove that the statement was false.

Fault Standard An element in defamation lawsuits that requires the plaintiff show that the publication of a statement was more than a simply mistake.

Federal Intelligence Surveillance Court A non-public court that is responsible with overseeing government warrants to surveil foreign national security risks in the United States.

First Sale Doctrine In copyright law, when consumers purchase a hard copy of a work, they own the hard copy as they would any other property.

Foreseeability In negligence law, defendants should have understood the chances that an injury may occur because of their actions.

Forum Doctrine Government can regulate based on where the speech takes place. There are four types of forums: traditional-public, designated-public, limited-public forum, and non-public forum.

Geotagging Geographic information attached to digital video, audio, pictures, posts, etc.

Haptic Gear Wearable technology that create the experience of touch.

Harassment Persistent behavior that threatens, intimidates, or alarms another person.

Hate Speech Speech aimed at a person based on their characteristics such as sex, gender, race, ethnicity, religion, etc. This is illegal in many parts of the world, but it is not in the United States.

Heckler's Veto The government must protect a speaker from a crowd that is attempting to shut down the speech.

Identification An element in defamation lawsuit that requires that the statement was about the plaintiff.

Incitement Unprotected speech that purposely calls others to commit a crime that likely occurred or did occur. Such speech can be punished criminally or civilly.

Indecency Sexually explicit material that is prohibited for certain audiences, venues, or times.

Infliction of Emotional Distress A tort law that allows recovery of damages for outrageous conduct that causes severe emotional distress.

Intellectual Property Original creations protected through copyright, trademark, or patent law.

Intent An element required for many crimes and torts. A person had to purposely commit the crime or tort.

Internet of Things The network of interconnected devices that can send and receive data through the internet.

Intrusion A tort that allows for recovery of damages for protects a physical invasion of one's privacy.

Involuntary Limited-Purpose Public Figure A controversy results in a person becoming a public figure.

Judicial Branch Interprets the laws (e.g., courts).

Legal Test A approach to settling a legal question involving steps or elements to be proven (e.g., 5 elements of defamation case).

Legislative Branch Creates the laws (e.g., Congress).

Libel per quod In defamation law, words that can only implicate a plaintiff when taken into context.

Libel per se In defamation law, certain words that automatically implicate a plaintiff (e.g., accusations of a crime).

Limited Public Forum The government has opened land for certain types of speech (e.g., classroom, auditorium). The government can regulate speech to serve the purpose of the forum.

Limited Purpose Public Figure In defamation law, they are plaintiffs who have thrust themselves to the forefront of a controversy. This usually has to be voluntary. They must prove actual malice.

Living Constitution A judicial philosophy that the U.S. Constitution (and other laws) need to evolve to fit current society.

Market Concentration The measure of how much control individual companies have in an industry.

Misappropriation of Likeness A commercial use of someone's image without their consent.

Modders A person who modifies video games and other technology at the code level.

Moot A case that is too late or no longer applies.

Native Advertising Advertising designed to look like content (e.g., an advertisement on Twitter that looks like a tweet).

Natural Monopoly A company that outlasts all competition by providing a better product preferred by consumers.

Negligence In tort law, when a party does not use reasonable care which leads to an injury.

Net Neutrality A policy that bars internet service providers from speeding up or slowing down sites and charging consumers different prices for the sites that they use.

Non-Public Forum Government land not open to public speech (e.g., prison). The government can regulate speech to serve the purpose of the forum.

Obscenity Sexual material that violates community norms and has no redeeming value.

Oligopoly When a few companies control most of the industry. This is legal in most cases under antitrust law.

Originalism A judicial philosophy of interpreting the Constitution and other laws through the lens of when it was passed.

Parallel Pricing Companies legally monitor competitor pricing and follow suit.

Patents In intellectual property law, they are protection for designs.

Perjury Knowingly lying while under oath.

Personal Property Tangible possessions that can be moved (e.g., phone or car).

Precedent Previous cases and legal tests. Courts use precedent to decide current cases.

Predatory Pricing A company sells its products at a great loss, in order to put competition out of business, so that it can control the market. It is illegal.

Preemption Federal government laws overrule state laws if the regulation is a power of the federal government.

Preponderance of Evidence The burden of proof in many civil lawsuits. Evidence is more in favor of one party (more than half).

Price Fixing Companies illegally collude to sell at high prices.

Prior Restraint Government censorship of speech before it occurs.

Probable Cause In criminal law, a person cannot arrest a person without a warrant unless there is good reason to believe that a crime has occurred.

Products Liability Negligence law pertaining to the manufacturer of goods.

Proximate Cause In negligence law, an action was part of the cause of the injury (even if not the direct cause).

Publication An element in defamation lawsuit that requires someone else besides the parties to have heard the statement.

Public Good A good that is judged to be vital to a society. Governments usually make sure that everyone has affordable access to such goods (e.g., utilities).

Public Interest, Convenience, and Necessity The requirement placed on broadcasters that have a federal license to operate a local radio or television station.

Puffery Exaggerations used by companies in advertising. Not considered to be false advertising.

Punitive Damages Jury awards that are meant to punish the defendant and deter others from doing the same (often large rewards).

Real Property Possessions that cannot be moved, such as land.

Reasonable Consumer Standard Used by government agencies to judge if a person would believe a claim made by a company in an advertisement.

Revenge Porn Sexually explicit photos or videos published without consent.

Rhetorical Hyperbole An exaggerated statement that is meant to make a certain point.

Right of Publicity The right to control and profit from the commercial use of one's image. Often called the celebrity's tort.

Right to be Forgotten Laws requiring search engines and other sites to scrub old data from searches.

Ripe A case cannot be brought to court before an injury.

Section 230 of the Communication Decency Act Federal law that generally immunes internet companies from liability for the actions of third parties on their sites.

Self-fulfilling Prophecy A prediction that leads to an expectation which changes our behavior toward making it come true.

Separation of Powers Each branch of government has a certain authority, and the other branches cannot exercise those powers.

SLAPS test In obscenity law, sexually explicit material is protected if it has serious literary, artistic, political, or scientific value.

Standing In order to sue, a party must have suffered an injury.

Statute A written law.

Strict liability A defendant is liable solely because an injury occurred, no matter the level of fault.

Summary Judgment A court can dismiss a case before a trial, if the facts asserted rise to a level of tort (e.g. defamation claim is over a true statement).

Surveillance Continued monitoring of a person or place.

Textualist—a person who relies strictly on the words of the law.

Time, Place, and Manner Restrictions U.S. governments are allowed to regulate the time, place, and manner of speech, so long as it is not based on the message or the speaker.

Tort An act that causes an injury that creates a legal liability.

Trademark Legal protections for the devices used by corporations to distinguish their goods (e.g., names, colors, slogans, etc.).

Traditional Public Forum Public lands that have been open to speech immemorial, such as sidewalks and parks. The government can regulate speech by time and manner.

Transformative Use/Artistic Relevance In copyright law and right to publicity, a person can use a protected work or image if they change it enough so it is now a new artistic work.

True Threats When a speaker expresses a serious intent to commit a crime against another.

Unprotected Speech Categories of speech that the U.S. Supreme Court has said fall outside the protections of free speech (e.g., copyright infringement, obscenity, true threats).

Vicarious Liability In negligence law, when a party is responsible for the actions of a third party (e.g. employer-employee relationship).

Virtual Reality (VR) A 3-dimensional environment created through computer graphics.

Virtue Ethics Using universal principles to guide decision making as to what is right or wrong.

Waivers of Liability In tort law, a contract (e.g., terms of agreement) that immune the party from legal responsibility.

References

Abbot, B. (2019, October 17). Youth suicide rate rises 56% in decade, CDC says. *Wall Street Journal*. https://www.wsj.com/articles/youth-suicide-rate-rises-56-in-decade-cdc-says-11571284861

Abrams, S. (2018, March 2). Persistent trouble with movie ratings. *Vanity Fair*. https://www.vanityfair.com/hollywood/2018/03/movie-ratings-mpaa-donald-trump

Abrams v. United States, 250 U.S. 616 (1919).

Ackerman, S. (2016, September 29). Snowden disclosures helped reduce use of Patriot Act provision to acquire email records. *The Guardian*. https://www.theguardian.com/us-news/2016/sep/29/edward-snowden-disclosures-patriot-act-fisa-court

Adler, A. (2001). Inverting the first amendment. *University of Pennsylvania Law Review, 149*, 921–1002. https://scholarship.law.upenn.edu/penn_law_review/vol149/iss4/1

Adler, J. (2015, July 8). The stare decisis court? *Reason*. https://reason.com/volokh/2018/07/08/the-stare-decisis-court

Allnutt, L. (October 17, 2011). *If the internet killed serendipity, it probably never existed anyway*. Radio Free Europe. https://www.rferl.org/a/if_the_internet_killed_serendipity_it_probably_never_existed_anyway/24361774.html

Almond, S. (2018, April 17). Want to stop fake news? Reinstate the fairness doctrine. *Boston Globe*. https://www.bostonglobe.com/opinion/2018/04/17/want-stop-fake-news-reinstate-fairness-doctrine/BpMw4D3s9qLrDwA2geLywN/story.html

Alterman, E. (2018, October 17). Why do the media keep parroting Donald Trump's falsehoods. *The Nation*. https://www.thenation.com/article/why-do-the-media-keep-parroting-trumps-falsehoods/

American Law Institute. (1965). *Restatement of the law, first, torts*. American Law Institute Publishers.

American Law Institute. (1977). *Restatement of the law, second, torts*. American Law Institute Publishers.

American Law Institute. (2010). *Restatement of the law, third, torts*. American Law Institute Publishers.

Anderson, M. (2017, May 11). *Twenty years on from Deep Blue vs. Kasparov: How a chess match started the big data revolution*. The Conversation. http://theconversation.com/twenty-years-on-from-deep-blue-vs-kasparov-how-a-chess-match-started the-big-data-revolution-76882

Anderson, M. (2017, March 17). *After 75 years, Isaac Asimov's Three Laws of Robotics need updating*. The Conversation. https://theconversation.com/after-75-years-isaac-asimovs-three-laws-of-robotics-need-updating-74501

Anderson, M. (2018, September 27). *A majority of teens have experienced some form of cyberbullying*. Pew Research Center. https://www.pewresearch.org/internet/2018/09/27/a-majority-of-teens-have-experienced-some-form-of-cyberbullying/

Anderton, K. (2019, March 21). Research report shows how much time we spend gaming. *Forbes.* https://www.forbes.com/sites/kevinanderton/2019/03/21/research-report-shows-how-much-time-we-spend-gaming-infographic/#7307e783e076

Apuzzo, M., & LaFranier, S. (2018, February 16). 13 Russians indicted as Mueller reveals effort to aid Trump campaign. *New York Times.* https://www.nytimes.com/2018/02/16/us/politics/russians-indicted-mueller-election-interference.html

Apuzzo, M., Sanger, D. E., & Schmidt, M. S. (2015, September 7). Apple and tech companies tangle with U.S. over access to data. *New York Times.* https://www.nytimes.com/2015/09/08/us/politics/apple-and-other-tech-companies-tangle-with-us-over-access-to-data.html

Armerding, T. (2018, December 20). *18 biggest data breaches of the 21st century.* CSO. https://www.csoonline.com/article/2130877/the-biggest-data-breaches-of-the-21st-century.html

Ashcroft v. American Civil Liberties Union, 535 U.S. 564 (2002).

Ashcroft v. Free Speech Coalition 535 U.S. 234 (2002).

Asimov, I. (1950). *I, Robot* (The Isaac Asimov Collection ed.). Doubleday.

Asimov, I. (1984). *The Complete Stories.* HarperCollins.

Asimov, I. (1985). *Robots and Empire,* Grafton Books.

Associated Press. (2019, June 4). Facebook, Google, Amazon and Apple face big tech anti-trust probe. *USA Today.* https://www.usatoday.com/story/tech/news/2019/06/04/facebook-google-amazon-and-apple-face-big-tech-antitrust-probe/1337395001

Associated Press (2020, March 17). Judge hands Katy Perry victory in "Dark Horse" copyright lawsuit. *Time.* https://time.com/5805463/katy-perry-dark-horse-court-judge-copyright/

Bacon, P. (2018, June 26). *Democrats are wrong about Republicans. Republicans are wrong about Democrats.* FiveThirtyEight. https://fivethirtyeight.com/features/democrats-are-wrong-about-republicans-republicans-are-wrong-about-democrats/

Bailis, P., Fachantidis, A., & Vlahavas, I. (2014). *Learning to play Monopoly: A reinforcement learning approach.* [Paper presentation]. The Society for the Study of Artificial Intelligence and Simulation of Behaviour 50th Annual Conference. London. http://doc.gold.ac.uk/aisb50/AISB50-S02/AISB50-S2-Bailis-paper.pdf

Balke, J. (2018, May 25). What's with all the privacy notices and website cookie notifications? *Houston Press.* https://www.houstonpress.com/news/why-are-you-seeing-privacy-notifications-online-all-of-a-sudden-10510337

Barkai, J., Kent, E., & Martin, P. (2006). Profile of a settlement. *Court Review, 42,* 34–38. http://aja.ncsc.dni.us/courtrv/cr42-3and4/CR42-3BarkaiKentMartin.pdf

Barnes, R. (2020, May 4). Supreme Court takes modest but historic step with teleconference hearings. *Washington Post.* https://www.washingtonpost.com/politics/courts_law/supreme-court-teleconference-hearings-bookingcom/2020/05/03/f5902bd6-8d76-11ea-a9c0-73b93422d691_story.html

Bartnicki v. Vopper, 532 U.S. 514 (2001).

Beaumont, T. & Price, M. (2019, September 14). Biden's 'record player' just 1 of his vintage references. *Associated Press.* https://apnews.com/857ff63c9dbd4ac9988f51a30df00f05

Beck, K. (2017, December 12). A hilarious new Harry Potter chapter was written by a predictive keyboard—and it's perfect. *Mashable.* https://mashable.com/2017/12/12/harry-potter-predictive-chapter/

Becker, J. M. (2014). Stories around the digital campfire: Fan fiction and copyright law in the age of the internet. *Connecticut Public Interest Law Journal, 14,* 133–155.

Beers, B. (2020, February 29). How Netflix pays for movie and TV show licensing. *Investopedia.* https://www.investopedia.com/articles/investing/062515/how-netflix-pays-movie-and-tv-show-licensing.asp

Belinchón, F., & Moynihan, R. (2018, July 25). 25 giant companies that earn more than entire countries. *Business Insider.* https://www.businessinsider.com/25-giant-companies-that-earn-more-than-entire-countries-2018-7

Bell, R. (2013, May 30). *Clearing up confusion about artisan food.* Michigan State University Extension. https://www.canr.msu.edu/news/clear

Bergman, S. (2017, February 28). We spend a billion hours a day on YouTube, more than Netflix and Facebook video combined. *Forbes.* https://www.forbes.com/sites/sirenabergman/2017/02/28/we-spend-a-billion-hours-a-day-on-youtube-more-than-netflix-and-facebook-video-combined/#63b2d53a5ebd

Berreby, D. (2017, March 3). Click to agree with what? No one reads terms of service, studies confirm. *The Guardian.* https://www.theguardian.com/technology/2017/mar/03/terms-of-service-online-contracts-fine-print

Bhagwat, A. (2018). Candidates and Cassandras: Technology and free speech on the Roberts court. *Washington University Law Review, 95,* 1327–1352. https://wustllawreview.org/volumes/95/issues/6/articles/2/

Blizzard. (2018, June 1). Blizzard end user agreement. https://www.blizzard.com/en-us/legal/fba4d00f-c7e4-4883-b8b9-1b4500a402ea/blizzard-end-user-license-agreement

Blumenthal, R. (1976, December 28). Death race. *New York Times,* 12. https://www.nytimes.com/1976/12/28/archives/death-race-game-gains-favor-but-not-with-the-safety-council.html

Bode, K. (2018, May 24). *America hates Comcast more than ever.* Vice. https://www.vice.com/en_us/article/7xmxza/america-hates-comcast-more-than-ever

Boliek, B. (2011, August 22). FCC finally kills off fairness doctrine. *Politico.* https://www.politico.com/story/2011/08/fcc-finally-kills-off-fairness-doctrine-061851

Bonasio, A. (2017, November 12). *Adidas vertical reality experience: Acrophobics need not apply.* VR Scout. https://vrscout.com/news/adidas-vertical-reality-experience-vr/

Bond, S. (2019, November 14). *Google's health data project under scrutiny.* NPR. https://www.npr.org/2019/11/14/779208282/google-health-data-project-under-scrutiny

Bond v. United States, 564 U.S. 211 (2011).

Boni-Saenz, A. (2007). Newsgathering in light of HIPAA. *Harvard Law Review, 120,* 1055–1066. http://scholarship.kentlaw.iit.edu/fac_schol/811

Bonnett, T. W. (2001). Is ISP-bound traffic local or interstate? *Federal Communication Law Journal, 53,* 239–287. https://www.repository.law.indiana.edu/fclj/vol53/iss2/3

Booten, J. (2015, July 26). Porn industry's billion dollar new frontier. *Forbes.* https://www.marketwatch.com/story/how-the-future-of-virtual-reality-depends-on-porn-2015-07-15

Boyle, M. (2012, September). Celebrity impersonation and the right of publicity. *John Marshall Review of Intellectual Property Law (Online).* https://ripl.jmls.edu/2012/09/18/celebrity-impersonation-and-the-right-of-publicity/

Bradshaw, T. (2018, March 29). Uber settles self-driving car crash case with victim's family. *Financial Times.* https://www.ft.com/content/1d7f174a-3362-11e8-b5bf-23cb17fd1498

Breslin, S. (2018, June 1). Porn's uncanny valley. *The Atlantic.* https://www.theatlantic.com/technology/archive/2018/06/porns-uncanny-valley/561521/

Brown, M. (2017, November 7). Stephen Hawking fears A.I. may replace humans, and he's not alone. *Inverse.com.* https://www.inverse.com/article/38054-stephen-hawking-ai-fears

Brown Shoe Co. v. U.S., 370 U.S. 294, 320 (1962).

Brown v. Board of Education, 347 U.S. 483 (1954).

Brown v. Entertainment Merchants Association, 564 U.S. 786 (2011).

Buchanan, K. (2016, June 10). When it comes to violence, does a PG-13 rating mean anything anymore? *Vulture.* https://www.vulture.com/2016/06/does-pg-13-rating-mean-anything-anymore.html?wpsrc=nymag

Buchleitner, J. (2018, April 5). *When virtual reality feels so real, so does the sexual harassment.* Reveal: The Center of Investigative Reporting. https://www.revealnews.org/article/when-virtual-reality-feels-real-so-does-the-sexual-harassment/

Burdeau v. McDowell, 256 U.S. 465, 475 (1921).

Burns, J. (2016, July 15). How the niche sex toy market grew into an unstoppable $15 billion market. *Forbes.* https://www.forbes.com/sites/janetwburns/2016/07/15/adult-expo-founders-talk-15b-sex-toy-industry-after-20-years-in-the-fray/#5fe71f935bb9

Byers v. Edmonson, 826 So. 2d 551, 553 (La. Ct. App. 2002).

Cakebread, C. (2017, November 15). You're not alone, no one reads terms of service agreements. *Business Insider.* https://www.businessinsider.com/deloitte-study-91-percent-agree-terms-of-service-without-reading-2017-11

California v. Ciraolo, 476 U.S. 207 (1986).

Campbell v. Acuff-Rose Music, Inc., 510 U.S. 560 (1994).

Caramore, M. B. (2008). Help! My intellectual property is trapped: Second Life, conflicting ownership claims and the problem of access. *Richmond Journal of Law & Technology,* 1–20. http://scholarship.richmond.edu/jolt/vol15/iss1/4

Carbone, C. (2019, May 29). *Facebook's average US user spent 38 minutes per day on the platform, a drop from 2017, but Instagram usage increased.* Fox News. https://www.foxnews.com/tech/facebooks-us-user-38-minutes-drop-from-2017

Castleman, M. (2016, November 3). Dueling statistics: How much of the internet is porn? *Psychology Today.* https://www.psychologytoday.com/us/blog/all-about-sex/201611/dueling-statistics-how-much-the-internet-is-porn

Caughill, P. (2017, September 14). *Researchers have linked a human brain to the internet for the first time ever.* Futurism. https://futurism.com/researchers-have-linked-a-human-brain-to-the-internet-for-the-first-time-ever

Center for American Progress. (January 23, 2012). *Americans agree: Corporations aren't people.* https://www.americanprogress.org/issues/courts/news/2012/01/23/11007/americans-agree-corporations-arent-people

Central Hudson Gas & Electric Corp. v. Public Service Commission, 447 U.S. 557 (1980).

Chakravorti, B. (2019, July 17). *3 myths to bust about breaking up big tech.* The Conversation. https://theconversation.com/3-myths-to-bust-about-breaking-up-big-tech-119283

Child Online Protection Act of 1998, 47 U.S.C. § 231 (1998).

Children's Online Privacy Protection Act of 1998 (COPPA) 15 U.S.C. § 6501–6506.

Chimel v. California, 395 U.S. 752 (1969).

Ciccatelli, A. (2018, February 26). *Intellectual property plays a big role in Silicon Valley deals.* IP Watchdog. https://www.ipwatchdog.com/2018/02/26/intellectual-property-plays-big-role-silicon-valley-deals/id=94010

Ciccone, A. (2012, August 7). *10 Ways to retaliate against bad customer service*. Huffington Post. https://www.huffpost.com/entry/ways-to-retaliate-against-bad-customer-service_n_1752383?guccounter=1&guce_referrer=aHR0cHM6Ly93d3cuZ29vZ2xlLmNvbS88&guce_referrer_sig=AQAAAIw943y45MeKOnp4Bxgqy5xeDqLDtDkClMU5__pB0NoFTc3bR_dJKRfjCgrdhZ9RudgW0hxQ4wVZ78YWfflNX4kpKW2HtMfLsK77h0_jfjCe52rB5TneL-Z2lxx_LgD28GP0n77PhSb5Z17Rnw6LcnLC7yeioE7AA7DVSnyW93Dsw

Citizens United v. Federal Election Commission, 558 U.S. 310 (2010).

Clifford, S. (2010, March 27). *High court rules corporations have right to bear arms* [Parody]. Huffington Post. https://www.huffpost.com/entry/high-court-rules-corporat_b_435619

Clifton, D. (2018, January 30). Russian trolls stoked anger over Black Lives Matter more than was previously known. *Mother Jones*. https://www.motherjones.com/politics/2018/01/russian-trolls-hyped-anger-over-black-lives-matter-more-than-previously-known/

Cohen, J. (2013, April 23). Memory implant. *Technology Review*. https://www.technologyreview.com/s/513681/memory-implants/

Coldeway, D. (2017, September 14). Facebook's generation of 'Jew Hater' and other advertising categories prompts system inspection. *TechCrunch*. https://techcrunch.com/2017/09/14/facebooks-generation-of-jew-hater-and-other-advertising-categories-prompts-system-inspection/

Coldry, N., & Mejias, U. (2019). *Costs of connection: How data is colonizing human life and appropriating it for capitalism*. Stanford University Press.

Communications Act of 1934, 47 U.S.C. § 151 (1934).

Communications Decency Act of 1996, 47 U.S.C. § 230, 233 (1996).

Congress wants to ban sex dolls that look like children. (2018, June 15). *Reason*. https://reason.com/blog/2018/06/15/congress-wants-to-ban-sex-dolls-that

Content rating. (n.d.) Wikipedia. https://en.wikipedia.org/wiki/Content_rating

Contractor suing homeowner over negative Yelp and Angie's list reviews. (2012, December 6). CBS News. https://www.cbsnews.com/news/contractor-suing-homeowner-over-negative-yelp-angies-list-reviews/

Contributions and Donations by Foreign Nationals, 52 U.S.C. § 30121 (2015).

Cook, J. (2019, April 8). Facebook plans to pass your photographs to advertisers and make users stars of online ads, patent reveals. *The Telegraph*. https://www.telegraph.co.uk/technology/2019/04/09/facebook-plans-pass-photographs-advertisers-make-users-stars/

Cooperation or resistance? The role of tech companies in government surveillance. (2018, May). *Harvard Law Review, 131*, 1722–1741. https://harvardlawreview.org/2018/04/cooperation-or-resistance-the-role-of-tech-companies-in-government-surveillance/

Copperweld Corp. v. Independence Tube Corp., 467 U.S. 752, 767 (1984).

Copyright Term Extension Act of 1998, Pub. L. No. 105–298 112 Stat. 2827 (1998).

Cortez, N. (2013). Do graphic tobacco warnings violate the first amendment? *Hastings Law Journal, 64*, 1467–1500. https://repository.uchastings.edu/hastings_law_journal/vol64/iss5/4

Countering illegal hate speech online. (2018, January 19). European Union Commission. http://europa.eu/rapid/press-release_MEMO-18-262_en.htm

Creasy, S. (2010). Defending against a charge of obscenity in the internet age: How Google searches can illuminate Miller's contemporary community standards. *Georgia State University Law Review, 26*, 1029–1059. t: https://readingroom.law.gsu.edu/gsulr/vol26/iss3/6

Crowley, M. (2014, November 10). Soul theft through photography. *Skeptical Briefs, Vol. 24.* https://www.csicop.org/sb/show/soul_theft_through_photography.

Crowther, B. T. (2012). (Un)reasonable expectation of digital privacy. *BYU Law Review, 2012*(1), 343–370. https://digitalcommons.law.byu.edu/lawreview/vol2012/iss1/7

Culhane, J. (2018, October 3). What happens if House Democrats vote to impeach Kavanaugh? *Politico.* https://www.politico.com/magazine/story/2018/10/03/democratic-house-impeach-kavanaugh-220921

Curbing Realistic Exploitative Electronic Pedophilic Robots (CREEPER) Act of 2018, 18 U.S.C. § 1462 HR 4665, 115th Congress (2018).

Dargin, M. (2017, May 18, 2017). Is protected health information safe in the cloud? *Network World.* https://www.networkworld.com/article/3197336/cloud-computing/is-protected-health-information-safe-in-the-cloud.html.

Darrah, N. (2018, August 30). *Jennifer Lawrence, Kate Upton's nude photo hacker sentenced to prison.* FOX News. http://www.foxnews.com/entertainment/2018/08/30/jennifer-lawrence-kate-uptons-nude-photo-hacker-sentenced-to-prison.html

Davidson v. Time Warner, Inc., No. Civ.A. V–94–006, 1997 WL 405907 at *12 (S.D. Tex. Mar. 311, 1997).

Davis, P. (2015, December 9). Sex in movies concerns U.S. parents more than violence, here's why. *Deseret News.* https://www.deseretnews.com/article/865643355/Sex-in-movies-concerns-US-parents-more-than-violence-Heres-why.html

Dee, J. (2000). Basketball Diaries, Natural Born Killers, and school shootings: Should there be limits on speech which triggers copycat violence? *Denver University Law Review, 77,* 713–737.

Del Valle, G. (2017, August 7). Most criminal cases end in plea bargains, not trials. *The Atlantic.* https://theoutline.com/post/2066/most-criminal-cases-end-in-plea-bargains-not-trials?zd=1&zi=urqi5qgk

Dennis, D. I. (2007). Obscenity law and its consequences in mid-nineteenth-century America. *Columbia Journal of Gender & Law, 16,* 43–86.

Department of Justice. (2018, July 31). Herfindahl–Hirschman index. https://www.justice.gov/atr/herfindahl-hirschman-index

DeSimone, M. T. (2018). Insta-famous: Challenges and obstacles facing bloggers and social media personalities in defamation cases. *Modern American, 11*(1), 77–101. https://digitalcommons.wcl.american.edu/tma/vol11/iss1/3

Desjardins, J. (2018, April 23). How Google retains more than 90% of the market share. *Business Insider.* https://www.businessinsider.com/how-google-retains-more-than-90-of-market-share-2018-4

Determann, L. (2018). No one owns data. *Hastings Law Journal, 70,* 1–43. http://www.hastingslawjournal.org/wp-content/uploads/70.1-Determann.pdf

Dewey, C. (2014, October 14). The only guide to Gamergate you will ever need to read. *Washington Post,* https://www.washingtonpost.com/news/the-intersect/wp/2014/10/14/the-only-guide-to-gamergate-you-will-ever-need-to-read/

Digital Media Law Project. (n.d.a). *State laws: Right to publicity.* http://www.dmlp.org/legal-guide/state-law-right-publicity

Digital Media Law Project. (n.d.b). *Using the name or likeness of another.* http://www.dmlp.org/legal-guide/using-name-or-likeness-another

Digital Millennium Copyright Act of 1998, Pub. L. 105–304. 112 Stat. 2860 (1998).

Disis, J. (2018, March 8). *The long history of blaming video games for violence*. CNN. https://money.cnn.com/2018/03/08/media/video-game-industry-white-house/index.html.

Dobbs, D. B. (2000). *The law of torts*. Westlaw.

Dougherty, M. (2018, September 21). *Controversy surrounds robot sex brothel set to open in Houston*. KHOU. https://www.khou.com/article/news/local/controversy-surrounds-robot-sex-brothel-set-to-open-in-houston/285-596991498

Duggan, M. (2014, October 22). *Online harassment*. Pew Research Center. http://www.pewinternet.org/2014/10/22/online-harassment/

Dunaway, J (2018). Watch Mark Zuckerberg squirm when a Congressman asks about the infamous Facemash. *Slate*. https://slate.com/technology/2018/04/rep-billy-long-asks-mark-zuckerberg-if-facebooks-predecessor-facemash-is-still-up-and-running.html

Duration of copyright: Works created on or after January 1, 1978. 17 U.S.C. § 302(b), 302(c) (2011).

Ehrenkranz, M. (2016, April 19). Virtual reality gamers are literally colliding with the physical world. *Business Insider*. https://www.businessinsider.com/virtual-reality-gamers-are-literally-colliding-with-the-physical-world-2016-4

Eimann v. Soldier of Fortune Magazine; 880 F.2d 830 (5th Cir. 1989).

Eisenach, J. A., & Kulick, R. (2019). Do state reviews of communications mergers serve the public interest? *Federal Communication Law Journal, 71*, 125–153. https://www.nera.com/content/dam/nera/publications/2019/71.2%E2%80%94Article-1%E2%80%94Jeffrey-Eisenach-and-Robert-Kulick.pdf

Eldred v. Ashcroft, 537 U.S. 186 (2003).

Elgammel, A. (2019, January). AI is blurring the definition of artist. *American Scientist*. https://www.americanscientist.org/article/ai-is-blurring-the-definition-of-artist.

Elgan, M. (2019, August 26). *Uh-oh! Silicon Valley is building a Chinese style social credit system*. Fast Company. https://www.fastcompany.com/90394048/uh-oh-silicon-valley-is-building-a-chinese-style-social-credit-system

Elonis v. United States, 138 S. Ct. 67, 199 L. Ed. 2d 21 (2017) (denying cert.).

Ernsburger, P. (2018, July 19). How does Netflix come up with recommendations for you, it actually a two-part trick. *Bustle*. https://www.bustle.com/p/how-does-netflix-come-up-with-recommendations-for-you-its-actually-a-two-part-trick-9679476

Everett, J., Pizarro, D., & Crockett, M. (2017, April 24). Why are we reluctant to trust robots. *The Guardian*. https://www.theguardian.com/science/head-quarters/2017/apr/24/why-are-we-reluctant-to-trust-robots

Ewalt, D. (2018, July 11). The first real boom in virtual reality? It's porn. *Wall Street Journal*. https://www.wsj.com/articles/the-first-real-boom-in-virtual-reality-its-pornography-1531320180

Ewing, E. (2017, April 7). Why authoritarians attack the arts. *New York Times*. https://www.nytimes.com/2017/04/06/opinion/why-authoritarians-attack-thearts.html?_r=0.

Exclusive rights in copyrighted works, 17 U.S.C. § 106(2) (2011).

Family Educational Rights and Privacy Act of 1974, 20 U.S.C. § 1232g; 34 CFR Part 99 (1974).

Federal Communications Commission. (n.d.). *Cable television*. https://www.fcc.gov/media/engineering/cable-television

Federal Communications Commission. (2017). *Broadcast ownership rules*. https://www.fcc.gov/sites/default/files/fcc_broadcast_ownership_rules.pdf

Federal Communications Commission v. FOX Television Stations, 567 U.S. 239 (2012).

Federal Communications Commission v. Pacifica Foundation, 438 U.S. 726 (1978).

Federal Trade Commission. (2015, December 22). *Enforcement policy statement on deceptively formatted advertisements.* https://www.ftc.gov/system/files/documents/public_statements/896923/151222deceptiveenforcement.pdf.

Federal Trade Commission. (2016, March 29). *FTC charges Volkswagen deceived consumers with its "clean diesel" campaign.* https://www.ftc.gov/news-events/press-releases/2016/03/ftc-charges-volkswagen-deceived-consumers-its-clean-diesel

Federal Trade Commission. (2017, April 19). *FTC reminds influencers and brands to clearly disclose relationship.* https://www.ftc.gov/news-events/press-releases/2017/04/ftc-staff-reminds-influencers-brands-clearly-disclose

Federal Trade Commission. (2019). *Predatory or below-cost pricing.* https://www.ftc.gov/tips-advice/competition-guidance/guide-antitrust-laws/single-firm-conduct/predatory-or-below-cost

File, P. (2017). Retract, expand: Libel law, the professionalization of journalism, and the limits of press freedom at the turn of the twentieth century. *Communication Law & Policy, 22,* 275–308. https://doi.org/10.1080/10811680.2017.1331623

First National Bank of Boston v. Bellotti, 435 U.S. 765 (1978).

Flowers, A. (2015, May 18). *Big business is getting bigger.* FiveThirtyEight. https://fivethirtyeight.com/features/big-business-is-getting-bigger

Food Lion v. Capital Cities/ABC, 194 F.3d 505 (5th Cir 1999).

Forsey, C. (2018, October 23). *5 ways augmented reality (AR) is transforming retail.* Hubspot. https://blog.hubspot.com/marketing/augmented-reality-retail

Fox v. Federal Communications Commission, 567 U.S. 239 (2012).

Foy, K. (2018, September 11). Artificial intelligence system uses transparent, human-like reasoning to solve problems. *MIT News.* http://news.mit.edu/2018/mit-lincoln-laboratory-ai-system-solves-problems-through-human-reasoning-0911.

Fried, I. (2019, April 11). *Facebook's forever war on misinformation.* Axios. https://www.axios.com/facebook-forever-war-misinformation-51fd819e-f048-4907-af47-dc4cb8d2a0ee.html

Frucci, A. (2010, February 12). *Steam powered vibrators and other terrifying early sex machines.* Gizmodo. https://gizmodo.com/5466997/the-steam-powered-vibrator-and-other-terrifying-early-sex-machines-nsfw

Gallagher, R. (2018, October 8). *Leaked transcript of private meeting contradicts Google's official story about China.* The Intercept. https://theintercept.com/2018/10/09/google-china-censored-search-engine/

Gardner, E. (2017, March 27). Will a class action over Pokémon GO redefine what it means to trespass? *Hollywood Reporter.* https://www.hollywoodreporter.com/thr-esq/will-a-class-action-pok-mon-go-redefine-what-means-trespass-989042

Gardner, E. (2019a, January 28). Purge producers escape lawsuit claiming rip off. *Hollywood Reporter.* https://www.hollywoodreporter.com/thr-esq/purge-producers-escape-lawsuit-claiming-rip-1180114

Gardner, E. (2019b, April 15). Will it soon be legal to say curse words on broadcast television? *Hollywood Reporter.* https://www.hollywoodreporter.com/thr-esq/will-it-soon-be-legal-say-curse-words-broadcast-television-1202050

Garfield, L. Y. (2011). The death of slander. *Columbia Journal of Law & the Arts, 35(1),* 17–56. 10.7916/D8BZ6GPT.

Gawker Media, LLC. v. Bollea, 170 So.3d 125 (Fla. 2d DCA 2015).

Gebhart, A. (2019, March 18). *Facial recognition: Apple, Amazon, Google and the race for your face.* CNET. https://www.cnet.com/how-to/facial-recognition-apple-amazon-google-and-the-race-for-your-face-facebook/

Gebhart, G., Cyphers, B., & Opsahl, K. (2018, September 13). *What we mean when we say data portability.* Electronic Frontier Foundation. https://www.eff.org/deeplinks/2018/09/what-we-mean-when-we-say-data-portability

Gellman, B., & Potras, L. (2013, June 7). U.S., British intelligence mining data from nine U.S. internet companies in broad secret program. *Washington Post.* https://www.washingtonpost.com/investigations/us-intelligence-mining-data-from-nine-us-internet-companies-in-broad-secret-program/2013/06/06/3a0c0da8-cebf-11e2-8845-970ccb04497-story.html?utm_term=.d4e8503565df

Gertz v. Robert Welch, Inc., 418 U.S. 323 (1974).

Geyer, P. & Wood, A. (2012). *The Cambridge Edition of the Works of Immanuel Kant.* London: Cambridge University Press.

Gill, K. (n.d.). *Visual guide: The balance of power between Congress and the presidency (1901–2017).* Wired Pen. https://wiredpen.com/resources/political-commentary-and-analysis/a-visual-guide-balance-of-power-congress-presidency/

Gill v. Whitford, 585 U.S. ____ (2017).

Gillespie, T. (2018). *Custodians of the internet: Platforms, content moderation, and the hidden decisions that shape social media.* Yale University Press.

Godfrey, E. (2017, July 27). Conservative groups fume over failed repeal votes. *The Atlantic.* https://www.theatlantic.com/politics/archive/2017/07/conservative-groups-fume-over-failed-repeal-votes/535017/

Golan v. Holder, 565 U.S. 302 (2012).

Gonzalez, D. (2015, July 25). *Mysterious deep web horror game Sad Satan has terrified and confused the internet.* Geek.com. https://www.geek.com/geek-cetera/mysterious-deep-web-horror-game-sad-satan-has-terrified-and-confused-the-internet-1626825/

Goodwin, M. (2018, June 27). *What's next for the reasonable expectation of privacy?* Slate. https://slate.com/technology/2018/06/after-the-supreme-courts-carpenter-ruling-where-is-the-reasonable-expectation-of-privacy-heading.html

Google. (n.d.). *About.* https://www.google.com/about/

Gostkowski v. Roman Catholic Church of the Sacred Hearts of Jesus & Mary, 186 N.E. 798, 800 (N.Y. 1933).

Graham, J. (2017, August 9). "You will get chipped- eventually." *USA Today.* https://www.usatoday.com/story/tech/2017/08/09/you-get-chipped-eventually/547336001/

Greenwald, G., Grim, R., & Gallagher, R. (2013, November 26). *Top-secret document reveals NSA spied on porn habits as part of plan to discredit "radicalizers."* Huffington Post. https://www.huffingtonpost.com/2013/11/26/nsa-porn-muslims_n_4346128.html

Griffe, A. (2017, October 1). *The list of 10 celebrities who ended up winning lawsuits will surprise you.* The JD Journal. https://www.jdjournal.com/2017/10/01/this-list-of-10-celebrities-who-ended-up-winning-lawsuits-will-surprise-you/

Griffin v. Wisconsin, 483 U.S. 868 (1987).

Griffiths, M. (2016, June 15) Gambling, sex and gaming in virtual reality. *Psychology Today.* https://www.psychologytoday.com/us/blog/in-excess/201606/gambling-sex-and-gaming-in-virtual-reality

Gurchiek, K. (2012, September 18). *Facial recognition technology raises privacy issues.* SHRM. https://blog.shrm.org/trends/facial-recognition-technology-raises-privacy-issues

Hanns Siedel Foundation (2019). *Influence of Russian disinformation operations: Specific examples in data and numbers.* https://www.europeanvalues.net/wp-content/uploads/2019/02/Influence-of-Russian-Disinformation-Operations-Specific-examples-in-data-and-numbers.pdf.

Harmon. A. G. (2011). Defamation in good faith: An argument for restating the defense of qualified privilege. *Barry Law Review, 16,* 27–56. t: https://lawpublications.barry.edu/barrylrcv/vol16/iss1/2

Harrell, E. (2019, January 23). Neuromarketing: What you need to know. *Harvard Business Review.* https://hbr.org/2019/01/neuromarketing-what-you-need-to-know

Harris v. Jones, 380 A.2d 611, 612 (Md. 1977).

Hart v. Electronic Arts, 717 F.3d 141 (3rd Cir. 2013).

Harwell, D. (2016, March 10). The creepy, inescapable advertisements that could define virtual reality. *Chicago Tribune.* https://www.chicagotribune.com/business/ct-virtual-reality-advertisements-wp-20160310-story.html

Hasselton, T. (2018, September 7). *Elon Musk: I'm about to announce a "Neuralink" product that connects your brain to computers.* CNBC. https://www.cnbc.com/2018/09/07/elon-musk-discusses-neurolink-on-joe-rogan-podcast.html

Haubursin, C. (2017, February 27). It's not you. Phones are designed to be addicting. *VOX.* https://www.vox.com/2018/2/27/17053758/phone-addictive-design-google-apple

Health Insurance Portability Privacy and Accountability Act of 1996, Pub. L. 104–19142 *U.S.C.* § 300gg and 29 *U.S.C* § 1181 et seq. and 42 *USC* 1320d et seq (1996).

Healy, M. (2018, December 20). Voters have high tolerance for politicians who lie, even those caught doing it. *Los Angeles Times.* https://www.latimes.com/science/sciencenow/la-sci-sn-fact-checking-politicians-20181218-story.html

Hegman, S. (2014, October 23). 40% of adults experience cyberbullying. *Adweek.* https://www.adweek.com/digital/new-study-finds-40-adults-cyberbullying/

Hentoff, D. (1992). *Freedom of speech for me, not for thee. How the American left and right relentlessly censor each other.* HarperCollins.

Herrman, J. (2017, December 5). The return of the techno-moral panic. *New York Times.* https://www.nytimes.com/2017/12/05/.../the-return-of-the-techno-moral-panic.html

Hern, A. (2019, February 14). New AI fake text generator may be too dangerous to release, say creators. *The Guardian.* https://www.theguardian.com/technology/2019/feb/14/elon-musk-backed-ai-writes-convincing-news-fiction

Hill, K. (2012, February 16). How Target figured out a teen girl was pregnant before her father did. *Forbes.* https://www.forbes.com/sites/kashmirhill/2012/02/16/how-target-figured-out-a-teen-girl-was-pregnant-before-her-father-did/#1f78d9236668

Hill v. Colorado, 530 U.S. 703 (2000).

Himes, J., & Song, T. (2019). Welcome to the Hotel California: The beast of algorithmic pricing. *Antitrust Chronicle.* https://www.competitionpolicyinternational.com/wp-content/uploads/2019/02/AC_February_1.pdf

Hobson, J. & McMahon, S. (2019, August 14). *Musician says Katy Perry's "Dark Horse" Copyright Case verdict sets dangerous precedent.* WBUR.org. https://www.wbur.org/hereandnow/2019/08/14/katy-perry-dark-horse-copyright-infringement-case

Honan, M. (2014, March 6). What Is doxing? *WIRED.* http://www.wired.com/2014/03/doxing/

How to tame the tech titans. (January 1, 2018). *The Economist.* https://www.economist.com/leaders/2018/01/18/how-to-tame-the-tech-titans

Howe, A. (n.d.). *Legal age of consent—All 50 states.* Survivor Alliance. https://www.thesurvivoralliance.com/forallies/legal-age-consent-50-states/

Hudson Jr., D. L. (n.d.). Miller test. *The first amendment encyclopedia.* https://www.mtsu.edu/first-amendment/article/1585/miller-test

Hustler Magazine, Inc. v. Falwell, 485 U.S. 46 (1988).

Illing, S. (2018, January 5). Why social media is terrible for multiethnic democracies. *VOX.* https://www.vox.com/policy-and-politics/2016/11/15/13593670/donald-trump-social-media-culture-politics

internet Movie Database. (n.d.). *Ready Player One—Quotes.* https://www.imdb.com/title/tt1677720

Irwin, J. (2017, July 28,). So long, Mii: The life and probable death of Nintendo's cartoon avatar. *Paste Magazine.* https://www.pastemagazine.com/articles/2017/07/so-long-mii-the-life-and-probable-death-of-nintend.html

Ivanova, I. (2018, April 10). 8 promises from Facebook after Cambridge Analytica. *CBS News.* https://www.cbsnews.com/news/facebooks-promises-for-protecting-your-information-after-data-breach-scandal/

Jaccarino, M. (2015, November 21). *Training simulation: Mass killers often share obsession with violent video games.* Fox News. https://www.foxnews.com/tech/training-simulation-mass-killers-often-share-obsession-with-violent-video-games

Jacobellis v. Ohio, 378 U.S. 184. (1964).

James v. Meow Media, Inc., 90 F. Supp. 2d 798 (W.D. Ky. 2000).

James v. Meow Media Inc., 300 F.3d 683 (6th Cir. 2002).

Jerome, J. W. (2013). Buying and selling privacy: Big data's different burdens and benefits. *Stanford Law Review Online, 66,* 47–53. https://review.law.stanford.edu/wp-content/uploads/sites/3/2016/08/66_StanLRevOnline_47_Jerome.pdf

Johnson, B. (2010, January 11). Privacy no longer a social norm, says Facebook founder. *The Guardian.* https://www.theguardian.com/technology/2010/jan/11/facebook-privacy

Johnston, I. (2017, April 13). AI robots learning racism, sexism and other prejudices from humans, study finds. *The Independent.* https://www.independent.co.uk/life-style/gadgets-and-tech/news/ai-robots-artificial-intelligence-racism-sexism-prejudice-bias-language-learn-from-humans-a7683161.html

Kang, C. (2018, August 28). Tech industry pursues a federal privacy law, on its own terms. *New York Times.* https://www.nytimes.com/2018/08/26/technology/tech-industry-federal-privacy-law.html

Karr, T. (2018, January 24) *Net neutrality violations: A brief history.* Free Press. https://www.freepress.net/our-response/expert-analysis/explainers/net-neutrality-violations-brief-history

Kastanek, A. D. (2014). From hit man to a military takeover of New York City: The evolving effects of Rice v. Paladin Enterprises on internet censorship. *Northwestern University Law Review, 99,* 383–436.

Katz v. United States, 389 U.S. 347 (1967).

Kaufman, B. (2017, November 18). *The next frontier for virtual reality: Courtrooms.* Bloomberg Law. https://biglawbusiness.com/the-next-frontier-for-virtual-reality-courtrooms/

Kearn, R. (2015, December 9). *Talking Barbie invades privacy, moms say.* Courthouse News Service. https://www.courthousenews.com/talking-barbie-invades-privacy-moms-say/

Keeton, P., & Prosser, W. L. (1984). *Prosser and Keeton on torts.* West Group.

Kelleher, K. (2018. July 5). Facebook reportedly apologizes after flagging Declaration of Independence as hate speech. *Fortune.* http://fortune.com/2018/07/05/facebook-apologizes-declaration-independence-hate-speech-racist-vindicator/

Khalil, A. (2005). *The Patriot Act and its infringement on civil liberties.* [Unpublished senior honors thesis] Eastern Michigan University. https://commons.emich.edu/cgi/viewcontent.cgi?referer=https://www.google.com/&httpsredir=1&article=1043&context=honors

Khana, D. (2014, January 26). *Disney works based on public domain.* Medium. https://medium.com/@derekkhanna/disney-works-based-on-public-domain-eb49ac34c3da

Kircher, J. J. (2007). The four faces of tort law: Liability for emotional harm. *Marquette Law Review, 90,* 789–920. https://scholarship.law.marquette.edu/cgi/viewcontent.cgi?article=1073&context=mulr

Killelea, E. (2017, October 11). 'Slender Man' trial: What's next for Morgan Geyser and Anissa Weier. *Rolling Stone.* https://www.rollingstone.com/culture/culture-features/slender-man-trial-whats-next-for-morgan-geyser-and-anissa-weier-115845/

Kirk, K. (2019, April 9). How Russia sows confusion in the U.S. vaccine debate. *Foreign Policy.* https://foreignpolicy.com/2019/04/09/in-the-united-states-russian-trolls-are-peddling-measles-disinformation-on-twitter/

Kluft, D. (2014, December 3). *Court rejects Glenn Becks limited purpose and involuntary public figure theories in marathon bombing defamation case.* Trademark and Copyright Law Blog. https://www.trademarkandcopyrightlawblog.com/2014/12/court-rejects-glenn-becks-limited-purpose-and-involuntary-public-figure-theories-in-marathon-bombing-defamation-case/

Knight First Amendment Institute v. Trump, No. 18-1691-cv (1st Cir. 2019).

Knorr, E. (2018, October 2). What is cloud computing? Everything you need to know. *Infoworld.* https://www.infoworld.com/article/2683784/cloud-computing/what-is-cloud-computing.html.

Komando, K. (2015, October 2). Three devices that are always listening and how to stop them. *USA Today.* https://www.usatoday.com/story/tech/columnist/komando/2015/10/02/3-gadgets-always-listening-and-how-stop-them/73191644/

Komando, K. (2015, December 22). Why you should say goodbye to Hello Barbie. *USA Today.* https://www.usatoday.com/story/tech/columnist/komando/2015/12/22/hello-barbie-hack-kim-komando/77636502/

Korematsu v. United States, 323 U.S. 214 (1944).

Kosseff, J. (2019). *Twenty-six words that created the internet.* Cornell Press.

Kramer, N., Sobieraj, S., Feng, D., Trubina, E., & Marsella, S. (2019). Being bullied in virtual environments: Expeirences and reactions of male and female students to male or female oppressor. In *The Impact of Virtual and Augmented Reality on Individuals and Society.* Eds. Slater, M., Sanchez-Vives, M. & Rizzo, A. Frontier Media.

Kreps, D. (2015). Tom Petty on Sam Smith settlement: No hard feelings, these things happen. *Rolling Stone.* https://www.rollingstone.com/music/music-news/tom-petty-on-sam-smith-settlement-no-hard-feelings-these-things-happen-35541/

Kumar, A., & Aizenman, N. C. (2011). Appeals court dismisses Virginia's health law challenge. *Washington Post.* Available at https://www.washingtonpost.com/national/health-science/appeals-court-dismisses-virginias-health-law-challenge/2011/09/08/gIQAB81xCK_story.html?utm_term=.d1ea609eb3da

Kyllo v. United States, 533 U.S. 27 (2001).

Lagasse, J. (2018, August 1). Healthcare spending near 20 percent of GDP, more than any other country. *Healthcare and Finance News*. https://www.healthcarefinancenews.com/news/healthcare-spending-near-20-percent-gdp-more-any-other-country

Laird, L. (2019, December 19). First amendment defense could threaten revenge pornography statutes. *ABA Journal*. https://www.abajournal.com/web/article/first-amendment-defense-claims-could-threaten-revenge-pornography-statutes

Lake, J. B. (2009). Restraining false light: Constitutional and common law limits on a "troublesome tort." *Federal Communication Law Journal, 61*, 625–650. https://www.repository.law.indiana.edu/fclj/vol61/iss3/4

Lake, J. (2017, February 19). Virtual reality exposure therapy for PTSD in the military. *Psychology Today*. https://www.psychologytoday.com/us/blog/integrative-mental-health-care/201702/virtual-reality-exposure-therapy-ptsd-in-the-military.

LaMotte, S. (2017, December 13). *The very real health dangers of virtual reality*. CNN. https://www.cnn.com/2017/12/13/health/virtual-reality-vr-dangers-safety/index.html

Lancaster, A. (2020, February 27). Snapchat not liable for how teens use speed filter, California Court rules. *Law.com*. https://www.law.com/therecorder/2020/02/27/snapchat-not-liable-for-how-teens-use-speed-filter-california-court-rules/?slreturn=20200312193809

Landau, S. (2019, March 22). *Is Section 215 no longer worth the effort?* Law Fare. https://www.lawfareblog.com/section-215-no-longer-worth-effort

Landi, H. (2016, October 5). *Study: Fitbit corporate wellness programs cut employer healthcare costs*. HCI Innovations Group. https://www.hcinnovationgroup.com/population-health-management/mobile-health-mhealth/news/13027550/study-fitbit-corporate-wellness-programs-cut-employer-healthcare-costs

Lapowsky, I., & Levy, S. (2018, April 24). Here's what Facebook won't let you post. *WIRED*. https://www.wired.com/story/heres-what-facebook-wont-let-you-post/

Larson III, R. (2013). Forgetting the first amendment: How obscurity-based privacy and a right to be forgotten are incompatible with free speech. *Communication Law & Policy, 18*, 91–120. https://doi.org/10.1080/10811680.2013.746140

Lawrence v. Texas, 539 U.S. 558 (2003).

Lee, T. (2018, January 8). *Why Mickey Mouse's 1998 extension probably won't happen again*. Ars Technica. https://arstechnica.com/tech-policy/2018/01/hollywood-says-its-not-planning-another-copyright-extension-push/

Leetaru. K. (2018, October 9). Can we finally stop terrorists from exploiting social media? *Forbes*. https://www.forbes.com/sites/kalevleetaru/2018/10/09/can-we-finally-stop-terrorists-from-exploiting-social-media/#7ec122b16d80.

Lenz v. Universal Music Corp., 801 F.3d 1126 (9th Cir. 2015).

Lessig, L. (2005). *Free culture: The future of creativity*. Penguin Books.

Li, T. (2018, August 7). China's influence on digital privacy could be global. *Washington Post*. https://www.washingtonpost.com/news/theworldpost/wp/2018/08/07/china-privacy/?utm_term=.fdd4b0eb7e18

Library of Congress. (n.d.) *America's first look into the camera: Daguerreotype portraits and views, 1839–1862*. http://www.loc.gov/teachers/classroommaterials/connections/daguerreotype/history.html

Liffreing, I. (2018, April 12). *How Bareburger is using AR on Snapchat to drive people to its restaurants*. Digiday. https://digiday.com/social/bareburger-using-ar-snapchat-drive-people-restaurants/

Little, B. (2016, December 19). Inside America's Shocking WWII Propaganda Machine. *National Geographic*. https://news.nationalgeographic.com/2016/12/world-war-2-propaganda-history-books/

Limitations on exclusive rights: Effect of transfer of particular copy or phonorecord, 17 U.S.C. § 109. (2011).

Limitations on exclusive rights: Fair use, 17 U.S.C. § 107 (2011).

Liptak, A. (2012, May 6). Are oral arguments worth arguing about? *New York Times*. https://www.nytimes.com/2012/05/06/sunday-review/are-oral-arguments-worth-arguing-about.html

Liquormart, Inc. v. Rhode Island, 517 U.S. 484 (1996).

Lopez, G. (2016, December 16). *What a lot of people get wrong about the infamous 1994 McDonald's hot coffee lawsuit*. VOX. https://www.vox.com/policy-and-politics/2016/12/16/13971482/mcdonalds-coffee-lawsuit-stella-liebeck

Lord, N. (2017, July 27). *The timeline of Ashley Madison hack*. Digital Guardian. https://digitalguardian.com/blog/timeline-ashley-madison-hack

Lorillard v. Reilly, 533 U.S. 525, 529 (2001).

Lovasz, A. (2017, July 13). *Content hungry consumers can tolerate a side dish of ads*. Marketing Dive. https://www.marketingdive.com/news/content-hungry-consumers-can-tolerate-a-side-dish-of-ads/446611

Lynskey, D. (2019, October 9). Alexa are you invading my privacy? The dark side of our voice assistants. *The Guardian*. https://www.theguardian.com/technology/2019/oct/09/alexa-are-you-invading-my-privacy-the-dark-side-of-our-voice-assistants

Mancini, J. (2018, September 13). Crazies at the social media barricades. *CMS Wire*. https://www.cmswire.com/digital-experience/crazies-at-the-social-media-barricades-unintended-consequences-and-next-steps/

Marr, B. (2018, May 5). How much data do we create everyday- the mind-blowing state everyone should read. *Forbes*. https://www.forbes.com/sites/bernardmarr/2018/05/21/how-much-data-do-we-create-every-day-the-mind-blowing-stats-everyone-should-read/#2e93f6ee6oba.

Marshall, A. (2018, July 17). *Health insurers are vacuuming up details about you and it could raise your rates*. NPR. https://www.npr.org/sections/health-shots/2018/07/17/629441555/health-insurers-are-vacuuming-up-details-about-you-and-it-could-raise-your-rates

Marton, K., Wilk, N., & Rogel, L. (2010). Protecting one's reputation—How to clear a name in world where name calling is so easy. *Phoenix Law Review, 4*, 52–82. *https://www.hg.org/legal-articles/protecting-one-s-reputation-how-to-clear-a-name-in-a-world-where-name-calling-is-so-easy-21477*

Masson v. New Yorker Magazine 501 U.S. 496 (1991).

Matsakis, L. (2018, September 14). Facebook's AI can scan memes, but can it understand them? *WIRED*. https://www.wired.com/story/facebook-rosetta-ai-memes/

Matthews, D. (2018, April 3). *Sinclair, the pro-Trump, conservative company taking over local news, explained*. Vox. https://www.vox.com/2018/4/3/17180020/sinclair-broadcast-group-conservative-trump-david-smith-local-news-tv-affiliate

May, G. (2017, May 17). Fifth Sense: The next stage of VR is total sensory immersion. *Wareable*. https://www.wareable.com/vr/senses-touch-taste-smell-immersion-7776

McCollum v. CBS, Inc., 249 Cal. Rptr. 187, (1988).

McCullen v. Coakley, 573 U.S. 464 (2014).

McDonald, H. (2018, November 4). *How 360 deals work in the music industry.* Balance Careers. https://www.thebalancecareers.com/how-360-deals-in-the-music-industry-work-2460343

McLaughlin, E. (2017, March 3). *Suspect OKs Amazon to hand over Echo recordings in murder case.* CNN. https://www.cnn.com/2017/03/07/tech/amazon-echo-alexa-bentonville-arkansas-murder-case/index.html

McMullen, G. (2015, September 16). *Content owners: Don't go crazy with takedown notices.* Medium. https://medium.com/truly-yours/content-owners-don-t-go-crazy-with-takedown-notices-ab396f550a21

Meek, A. (2019, January 31). *Netflix usage passed cable and satellite for the first time in 2018.* BGR. https://bgr.com/2019/01/31/netflix-vs-cable-2018-statistics

Meiklejohn, A. (1948). *Free speech and its relation to government.* Harper Brothers.

Mejias, U., & Vokuev, N. (2018). Disinformation and the media: The case of Russia and Ukraine. *Media, Culture and Society, 30,* 1027–1042. https://doi.org/10.1177/0163443716686672.

Miami Herald Publishing Co. v. Tornillo, 418 U.S. 241(1974).

Milkovich v. Lorain Journal Co., 497 U.S. 1 (1990).

Miller v. California, 413 U.S. 15 (1972).

Morris, D. (2018, August 11). Man who stole Alaska airline plane said he was "just a broken guy." *Fortune.* http://fortune.com/2018/08/11/alaska-air-plane-thief-sea-tac/

Mtima, L. (2012). What's mine is mine but what's yours is ours: IP imperialism, the right of publicity, and intellectual property social justice in the digital information age. *Arizona State Sports & Entertainment Law Journal, 2,* 323–388. https://scholar.smu.edu/scitech/vol15/iss3/2/

Mulrooney, T.B. (2012). A critical examination of New York's right of publicity claim. *St. John's Law Review, 74,* 1139–1166. https://scholarship.law.stjohns.edu/cgi/viewcontent.cgi?article=1457&context=lawreview

Nader v. General Motors Corp. 307 N.Y.S.2d 647 (N.Y. 1970).

Nakashima, R. (2018, August 13). Google tracks your movements, like it or not, AP investigation finds. *USA Today.* https://www.usatoday.com/story/tech/news/2018/08/13/google-tracks-your-movements-ap-investigation/976463002/

Nation Magazine v. U.S. Department of Defense, 762 F. Supp. 1558 (S.D.N.Y. 1991).

National Socialist Party of America v. Village of Skokie, 432 U.S. 43 (1977).

Near v. Minnesota, 283 U.S. 697 (1931).

New York Times News Service (1976, December 28). "Death race": Cartoon or morbid? *The Post-Crescent.* A-1. https://www.newspapers.com/newspage/288123577/

New York Times Co. v. Sullivan, 376 U.S. 254, 256 (1964).

New York Times Co. v. United States, 403 U.S. 713 (1971).

New York v. Ferber, 458 U.S. 747 (1982).

Ngan, M. (2018, August 23). *Get smart: Are you equipped for the next workplace revolution?* Business World. http://www.bworldonline.com/get-smart-are-you-equipped-for-the-next-workplace-revolution/

Nguti, T. (1986). Patent law: doctrinal stability—A research and development definition of invention is key. *Valparaiso University Law Review, 20,* 653–703. https://scholar.valpo.edu/cgi/viewcontent.cgi?article=1541&context=vulr

Nickerson v. Hodges, 84 So. 37, 38–39 (La. 1920)

Nield, D. (2017, October 30). *Who actually owns your content when you post it to the web.* Gizmodo. https://gizmodo.com/who-actually-owns-your-content-when-you-post-it-to-the-1819953868

Nielsen Research Group (2018, July 31). *Time flies: U.S. adults spend nearly half a day interacting with media.* Nielsen. https://www.nielsen.com/us/en/insights/article/2018/time-flies-us-adults-now-spend-nearly-half-a-day-interacting-with-media/

NOLO. (n.d.). *Personal jurisdiction: In court can I sue a defendant?* https://www.nolo.com/legal-encyclopedia/personal-jurisdiction-where-sue-defendant-29560.html

Norwood v. Soldier of Fortune Magazine, 651 F.Supp. 1397 (W.D. Ark. 1987).

Now you can virtually drive a Volvo with Google Cardboard. (2014). *Ad Age.* https://adage.com/creativity/work/volvo-reality-test-drive-teaser/37842

Noyes, K. (2015, July 1). VPN users beware—you may not be as safe as you think you are. *PC World.* https://www.pcworld.com/article/2943472/vpn-users-beware-you-may-not-be-as-safe-as-you-think-you-are.html

Nutrient content claims for fat, fatty acid, and cholesterol content of foods, 21 CFR 101.62. (2012).

O'Connor, A. E. (2011). Access to media all-a-twitter: Revisiting Gertz and the access to media test in the age of social networking. *Federal Communication. Law Journal, 63*(2), 507–534. https://www.repository.law.indiana.edu/cgi/viewcontent.cgi?article=1591&context=fclj

O'Dowd, P. (2018, December 21). *As facial recognition booms, so do privacy concerns.* WBUR. https://www.wbur.org/hereandnow/2018/12/21/facial-recognition-privacy-concerns

O'Malley, K. (November 21, 2017). Jennifer Lawrence explains why she didn't sue over nude photo leak scandal. *Elle.* https://www.elle.com/uk/life-and-culture/culture/news/a40104/jennifer-lawrence-why-she-didnt-sue-nude-photo-leak-scandal/

Oremus, W. (2013, August 20). *Kagan admits Supreme Court justices haven't quite figured out email yet.* Slate. http://www.slate.com/blogs/future_tense/2013/08/20/elena_kagan_supreme_court_justices_haven_t_gotten_to_email_use_paper_memos.html

Owen, D., & Davis, M. (2014). *Madden and Davis on products liability, 4th ed.* Thomson-West.

Palmer, S. (2018, January 22). Facebook: Ministry of truth? *Ad Age.* https://adage.com/article/digitalnext/facebook-ministry-truth/312033

Paquette, J. (2017). Old is not always wise: The inapplicability of the Sherman act in the age of the internet. *Temple Law Review Online, 89,* 1–43. https://www.templelawreview.org/lawreview/assets/uploads/2017/08/Paquette-89-Temp.-L.-Rev.-Online.pdf

Pasquale, F. (2016, October 18, 2016). Get off the trolley problem. *Slate.* http://www.slate.com/articles/technology/future_tense/2016/10/self_driving_cars_shouldn_t_have_to_choose_who_to_protect_in_a_crash.html.

Pawlyk, O. (2019). Air Force's future stealthy combat drone could use AI learning . *Military News.* https://www.military.com/daily-news/2019/06/20/air-forces-future-stealthy-combat-drone-could-use-ai-learn.html

Perez, S. (2016, March 8). *Controversial people rating app Peeple goes live, has a plan to profit from users' negative reviews.* Tech Crunch. https://techcrunch.com/2016/03/08/controversial-people-rating-app-peeple-goes-live-has-a-plan-to-profit-from-users-negative-reviews/

Perry, A. M. (2003). Guilt by saturation: Media liability for third-party violence and the availability heuristic. *Northwestern University Law Review, 97,* 1045–1073.

Perry Education Association v. Perry Local Educators, 460 U.S. 37 (1983).

Perzanowski, A., & Jason Schultz, J. (2018). *End of ownership: Personal property in the digital economy.* MIT Press.

Pierson, D. (2018, August 23). We now know Russia isn't the only foe that's learned to exploit U.S. social media. *Los Angeles Times.* http://www.latimes.com/business/technology/la-fi-tn-facebook-iran-20180822-story.html

Plaugic, L. (2017, December 19). *YouTube reportedly signs new music licensing deals with UMG and Sony Music.* The Verge. https://www.theverge.com/2017/12/19/16796058/youtube-universal-music-group-sony-agreement-royalties

Politico. (2018, October 6). *Is Kavanaugh damaged goods?* https://www.politico.com/magazine/story/2018/10/06/kavanaugh-confirmation-reaction-221087

Politifact. (n.d.). *Donald Trump.* Politifact: The Poytner Institute. https://www.politifact.com/personalities/donald-trump/

Pope v. Illinois, 481 U.S 497 (1987).

Posetti, J., & Matthews, A. (2018, July). *A short guide to the history of "fake news" and disinformation.* International Commission of Jurists. https://www.icfj.org/sites/default/files/2018-07/AShortGuidetoHistoryofFakeNewsandDisinformation_ICFJFinal.pdf

Presttito, R. (2007, November 20). *The birth of the administrative state- where it came from and what it means for limited government.* Heritage Foundation. https://www.heritage.org/political-process/report/the-birth-the-administrative-state-where-it-came-and-what-it-means-limited.

Pridmore, J., & Overocker, J. (2014). Privacy in virtual worlds: A U.S. perspective. *Journal of Virtual Worlds Research, 7,* 1–14. https://doi.org/10.4101/jvwr.v7i1.7067.

Pritchard, M. (2018, September 24). *Will Democrats regret weaponizing judiciary?* Politico. https://www.politico.com/magazine/story/2018/09/24/democrats-weaponize-judiciary-220530.

Prosser, W. L. (1964). *Handbook of the law of torts.* West.

PROTECT Act of 2003, 18 U.S.C. § 1466A. (2003).

Protect America Act of 2007, Pub. L. No. 110–55, 121 Stat. 552 (2007).

Radio Act of 1927, 47 U.S.C. § 4. (1927).

Raustiala, K., & Sprigman, C. (2012, January 12). *How much do music and movie piracy really hurt the U.S. economy.* Freakonomics Blog. http://freakonomics.com/2012/01/12/how-much-do-music-and-movie-piracy-really-hurt-the-u-s-economy/

Ready, F. (2019, January 25). *EU's right to be forgotten could come under heavy challenge.* Law.com. https://www.law.com/legaltechnews/2019/01/15/eus-right-to-be-forgotten-could-come-under-heavy-challenge/?slreturn=20190619135040

Red Lion Broadcasting Co. v. Federal Communications Commission, 395 U.S. 367 (1969).

Reed, A., & Samuelson, J. (2017, February 7). When do consumer boycotts work? *New York Times.* https://www.nytimes.com/roomfordebate/2017/02/07/when-do-consumer-boycotts-work

Render, M. (2017). The concept of property. *University of Pittsburgh Law Review, 78,* 437–492. https://lawreview.law.pitt.edu/ojs/index.php/lawreview/article/view/497/345

Reno v. American Civil Liberties Union, 521 U.S. 844 (1997).

Rice v. Paladin Enterprise, 128 F.3d 233, 233 (4th Cir. 1997).

Richards, J. (2016, July 11). Most Americans still believe in free speech, but don't know much about it. *Washington Examiner.* https://www.washingtonexaminer.com/most-americans-still-believe-in-free-speech-but-dont-know-much-about-it.

Rienzi, M. L., & Buck, S. (2002). Federal courts, overbreadth, and vagueness: Guiding principles for constitution challenges to uninterrupted state statutes. *Utah Law Review 2002*, 381–471.

Rifken, R. (2016, January 20). *Majority of Americans dissatisfied with corporate influence*. Gallup. https://news.gallup.com/poll/188747/majority-americans-dissatisfied-corporate-influence.aspx

Robbins Collection. (2010). *The common law and civil tradition*. Berkeley Law, University of California. https://www.law.berkeley.edu/research/the-robbins-collection/exhibitions/common-law-civil-law-traditions/

Roberts, J. J. (2019, August 28). AOC blocking twitter users. *Fortune*. https://fortune.com/2019/07/10/aoc-sued-twitter-trump-lawsuit/

Robson, J. (2013). *The Collected Works of John Stuart Mill*. Routledge.

Rocha, V. (2016, July 14). 2 California men fall of edge of ocean blue bluff while playing Pokemón GO. *Los Angeles Times*. http://www.latimes.com/local/lanow/la-me-ln-pokemon-go-players-stabbed-fall-off-cliff-20160714-snap-story.html.

Root, D. (2020, January 16). Precedent matters at the Supreme Court—until it doesn't. *Reason*. https://reason.com/2020/01/16/precedent-matters-at-the-supreme-court-until-it-doesnt/

Rosenzweig, P. (2004). Civil liberty and the response to terrorism. *Duquesne Law Review, 42*, 663–723.

Rosini, N. (1991). *The practical guide to libel law*. Praeger.

Roth v. United States. 354 U.S. 476 (1957).

Rowland, L. & Goodman, R. (2016, March 15). *Is it okay to kick people out of campaign rallies? That depends*. ACLU. https://www.aclu.org/blog/free-speech/it-okay-kick-people-out-campaign-rallies-depends

Ruccho v. Common Cause 588 U.S. ___ (2019).

Salam, M., & Stack, L. (2018, February 23). Do video games lead to mass shootings? Researchers say no. *New York Times*. https://www.nytimes.com/2018/02/23/us/politics/trump-video-games-shootings.html

San Mateo v. Southern Pacific Railroad, 116 U.S. 138 (1885).

Santos, A. A. (2018, September 24). *Nike's Colin Kaepernick ad sparked a boycott—and earned $6 billion for Nike*. Vox. https://www.vox.com/2018/9/24/17895704/nike-colin-kaepernick-boycott-6-billion

Sarver v. Chartier, 813 F.3d 891 (9th Cir. 2016).

Sawyer, B., & Cox, C. (2018, December 27). *How does health spending in the U.S. compare to other countries?* Health System Tracker. https://www.healthsystemtracker.org/chart-collection/health-spending-u-s-compare-countries/

Schenck v. U.S., 249 U.S. 47 (1919).

Schneier, B. (2013, June 6). What we don't know about spying on citizens: Scarier than what we know. *The Atlantic*. https://www.theatlantic.com/politics/archive/2013/06/what-we-dont-know-about-spying-on-citizens-scarier-than-what-we-know/276607/

Schonfeld, Z. (2015, September 19). Parental advisory forever: An oral history on the PMRC's war on dirty lyrics. *Newsweek*. https://www.newsweek.com/2015/10/09/oral-history-tipper-gores-war-explicit-rock-lyrics-dee-snider-373103.html

Schwartz, O. (2018, December 4). Are Google and Facebook really suppressing conservative politics? *The Guardian*. https://www.theguardian.com/technology/2018/dec/04/google-facebook-anti-conservative-bias-claims

Sciliano, R. (2019, January 4). *Identity theft crimes by the numbers*. The Balance. https://www.thebalance.com/identity-theft-crimes-by-the-numbers-4157714

Scotusblog. (n.d.). *Court procedure*. http://www.scotusblog.com/reference/educational-resources/supreme-court-procedure/

Sebelius v. Hobby Lobby, 134 S. Ct. 678 (2013).

Seeley, T. (2018, July 5). Online kids' game Roblox shows female character being violently gang raped, mom warns. *USA Today*. https://www.usatoday.com/story/life/allthemoms/2018/07/05/roblox-kids-game-character-sexually-violated/759690002/

Segal, L. (2015, September 8). *Pastor outed on Ashley Madison commits suicide*. CNN. https://money.cnn.com/2015/09/08/technology/ashley-madison-suicide/index.html

Senagore, A. J. (2010). The benefits of limiting strict liability for used-product sellers. *Northern Illinois University Law Review, 30*, 349–385. https://commons.lib.niu.edu/bitstream/handle/10843/20518/30-2-349-Senagore-pdfA.pdf?sequence=1&isAllowed=y

Shafer, J. (2007, January 10). *The whole story about that toxic spill and Clear Channel monopoly*. Slate. https://slate.com/news-and-politics/2007/01/the-whole-story-about-that-toxic-spill-and-the-clear-channel-monopoly.html

Shapiro, A. (2009, June 23). *Conservatives have "originalism;" Liberals have...?* NPR. https://www.npr.org/templates/story/story.php?storyId=105439966

Sharma, M. (2014). Advergaming—The novel instrument in the advertising. *Procedia Economics & Finance, 11*, 247–254. https://core.ac.uk/download/pdf/82195757.pdf

Sherman Antitrust Act of 1890, 15 U.S.C. § 1 *et seq*. (1890).

Shiff, A. (2018, May 4). Twitter has a big problem in Southeast Asia: Bots before the ballot in Malaysia and beyond. *Time*. http://time.com/5260832/malaysia-election-twitter-bots-social-media/

Shoenberger, A. E. (2010). Connecticut Yankee speech in Europe's court: An alternative vision of constitutional defamation law to New York Times Co. v. Sullivan? *Quinnipiac Law Review, 28*, 431–489. https://lawecommons.luc.edu/cgi/viewcontent.cgi?article=1083&context=facpubs

Shontell, A. (2011, January 18). *15 weirdly effective places to advertise you've never thought of*. Business Insider. https://www.businessinsider.com/15-weirdly-effective-places-to-advertise-youve-never-thought-of-2011-1

Silverman, C. (2018, April 17). *How to spot a deepfake like the Barack Obama–Jordan Peele video*. Buzzfeed. https://www.buzzfeed.com/craigsilverman/obama-jordan-peele-deepfake-video-debunk-buzzfeed

Simon & Schuster v. Crime Victims Board, 502 U.S. 105 (1991).

Simpson, J. (2017, January 2). Washing machine will turn detective. *The Times*. https://www.thetimes.co.uk/article/washing-machine-will-turn-detective-djq3ojdff?wgu=270525_542 64_15593271097785_6af05ffdd2&wgexpiry=1567103109&utm_source=planit&utm_medium=affiliate&utm_content=22278

Sleyukh, A. (2016, April 28). *Yahoo's security chief on encryption debate: What is the greater good*. NPR. https://www.npr.org/sections/alltechconsidered/2016/04/28/475883338/yahoos-security-chief-on-encryption-debate-what-is-the-greater-good

Snyder v. Phelps, 562 U.S. 443, 458 (2011).

Society for the Propagation of the Gospel in Foreign Parts v. The Town of New Haven, 21 U.S. 464 (1823).

Somani, M. (2018, May 11). *Connect the dots: IoT security risks in an increasingly connected world.* Security Intelligence. https://securityintelligence.com/connect-the-dots-iot-security-risks-in-an-increasingly-connected-world/

Sorrell v. IMS Health Inc., 564 U.S. 552 (2011).

Statista. (2020). *Estimated VR device shipment share by vendor worldwide in 2018 and 2019.* https://www.statista.com/statistics/755645/global-vr-device-market-share-by-vendor/

Steenson, M. (2014). Presumed damages in defamation law. *William Mitchell Law Review, 40*(4), 1492–1542. http://open.mitchellhamline.edu/wmlr/vol40/iss4/9

Sterling, B. (2019, March 15). The big 9 G-MAFIA BAT. *WIRED.* /https://www.wired.com/beyond-the-beyond/2019/03/big-nine-g-mafia-bat

Stewart, J. (2015, April). *Can legislation stop cybercrime?* Computer Weekly. https://www.computerweekly.com/opinion/Can-legislation-stop-cyber-crime

Streitfeld, D. (2018, October 18). Computer stories: A.I. is beginning to assist novelists. *New York Times.* https://www.nytimes.com/2018/10/18/technology/ai-is-beginning-to-assist-novelists.html

Stucke, M., & Grunes, A. (2001). Antitrust and the marketplace of ideas. *Antitrust Law Journal, 69,* 249–302. https://www.jstor.org/stable/40843516?seq=1#metadata_info_tab_contents

Subject matter of copyright: Compilations and derivative works. 17 U.S.C. § 102, 103 (2012).

Sullivan, M. (2018, November 29). *The 1996 law that made the web is in the crosshairs.* Fast Company. https://www.fastcompany.com/90273352/maybe-its-time-to-take-away-the-outdated-loophole-that-big-tech-exploits

Susan B. Anthony List v. Driehaus, 814 F. 466 (6th Cir. 2016).

Tang, J., Liu, Y., Hu, D., & Zhou, Z. (2018). Towards BCI-actuated smart wheelchair system. *Biomedical engineering online, 17*(1), 111. https://doi.org/10.1186/s12938-018-0545-x

Taylor, K. R. (2014). Anything you post online can and will be used against you in a court of law: Criminal liability and first amendment implications of social media expression. *National Lawyers Guild Review. 71.* 78–106. https://www.nlg.org/nlg-review/wp-content/uploads/sites/2/2016/11/NLGRev-71-2-Final.pdf

Taylor, S. (2005). Small hope floats: How the lower courts have sunk the right of privacy. *West Virginia Law Review, 108,* 459–500.

Terry v. Ohio, 392 U.S. 1 (1968).

Thomson-DeVeaux, A. (2018, May 29). *The Supreme Court is stubbornly analog, by design.* FiveThirtyEight. https://fivethirtyeight.com/features/the-supreme-court-is-stubbornly-analog-by-design/

Thomson-DeVeaux, A., & Roeder, O. (2018, October 1). *Is the Supreme Court facing a legitimacy crisis.* FiveThirtyEight. https://fivethirtyeight.com/features/is-the-supreme-court-facing-a-legitimacy-crisis/

Tiffany, K. (2018, October 23). *No industry is weirder than the dead celebrity hologram industry.* Vox. https://www.vox.com/the-goods/2018/10/23/18010274/amy-winehouse

Tiku, N. (2018, March 19). Europe's new privacy law will change the web and more. *WIRED.* https://www.wired.com/story/europes-new-privacy-law-will-change-the-web-and-more/

Titlow, J. (2016, July 13). *YouTube is using AI to police copyright to the tune for $2 billion payouts.* Fast Company. https://www.fastcompany.com/4013603/youtube-is-using-ai-to-police-copyright-to-the-tune-of-2-billion-in-payouts

Top 10 scary deepfake videos. (2019). YouTube. https://www.youtube.com/watch?v=5t02JfpGfcQ&t=17s

Trammell, K. (2018). Blade Runner predicted life would be like in 2019. Here's what movie got right- and wrong. *CNN.* https://www.cnn.com/2018/12/28/movies/blade-runner-predictions-2019-trnd/index.html

Trump v. Hawaii, 585 U.S. ____ (2018).

Turner Broadcasting v. Federal Communications Commission, 512 U.S. 622 (1994).

Twitter suspensions. (n.d.), Wikipedia. https://en.wikipedia.org/wiki/Twitter_suspensions

Tyson, G. (2018, August). *The rise of cyberlockers: How online piracy is fighting back.* The Conversation. https://theconversation.com/the-rise-of-cyberlockers-how-online-piracy-is-fighting-back-101162

United States Foreign Intelligence Surveillance Court. (n.d.). *About the court.* https://www.fisc.uscourts.gov/about-foreign-intelligence-surveillance-court

United States v. Alvarez, 567 U.S. 709 (2012).

United States v. E. I. du Pont de Nemours & Co., 351 U.S. 377, 387–94 (1956).

United States v. Grinnell Corp., 384 U.S. 563, 570–71 (1966).

United States v. Handley, 564 F. Supp. 2d 996 (S.D. Iowa 2008).

United States v. Jones, 565 U.S. 400 (2012).

United States v. Microsoft Corporation, 253 F.3d 34 (D.C. Cir. 2001).

United States v. Stevens, 559 U.S. 460 (2010).

Usman, J. O. (2014). Finding the lost involuntary public figure. *Utah Law Review, 2014.* 951–1012. https://dc.law.utah.edu/cgi/viewcontent.cgi?article=1232&context=ulr

U.S. Const. amend. I.

U.S. Copyright Office. (n.d.) *A brief history.* https://www.copyright.gov/timeline/

U.S. Copyright Office (2019). *Authors, attribution, and integrity: Examining moral rights in the United States.* https://www.copyright.gov/policy/moralrights/full-report.pdf

U.S. Department of Education (2007, October). *Parents' guide to the* Family Educational Rights and Privacy Act: *Rights regarding children's education records.* https://www2.ed.gov/policy/gen/guid/fpco/brochures/parents.html

U.S. Patriot Act of 2001, Pub. L. No. 107–56, 115 Stat. 272 (2001).

Vanian, J. (2018, June 25). Unmasking A.I.'s bias problem. *Fortune.* http://fortune.com/longform/ai-bias-problem/

Varsave, N. (2019). The role of dissents in the formation of precedent. *Duke Journal of Constitutional Law & Public Policy, 14,* 286–342

Viacom International, Inc. v. YouTube, Inc., 676 F.3d 19, 26 (2d Cir. 2012).

Victor, D. (2016, March 24). Microsoft created a twitter bot to learn from user—it quickly became a racist jerk. *New York Times.* https://www.nytimes.com/2016/03/25/technology/microsoft-created-a-twitter-bot-to-learn-from-users-it-quickly-became-a-racist-jerk.html

Viney, S. (2016). *What is the dark net and how will it shape the digital age.* Australia Broadcasting Company. http://www.abc.net.au/news/2016-01-27/explainer-what-is-the-dark-net/7038878

Vinyard, N. M. (2016). Extralegal factors and the imposition of lifetime supervised release for child pornography offenders. *Federal Probation, 80,* 45–57. https://www.uscourts.gov/sites/default/files/80_1_6_0.pdf

Virelli III, L. J. (2014). Deconstructing arbitrary and capricious review. *North Carolina Law Review, 92,* 721.

Virginia State Pharmacy Board v. Virginia Citizens Consumer Council, 425 U.S. 748 (1976).

Virginia v. Black, 538 U.S. 343, 359 (2003).

Voting and Elections, 52 U.S.C. § 30121 (2002).

Votruba, A. M. (2013). Will the real reasonable person please stand up? Using psychology to better understand how juries interpret and apply the reasonable person standard. *Arizona State Law Journal, 45,* 703–732. https://digitalcommons.unl.edu/cgi/viewcontent.cgi?article=1909&context=psychfacpub.

Waldman, A. E. (2012). Tormented: Antigay bullying in schools. *Temple Law Review, 84,* 385–459. https://heinonline.org/HOL/Page?handle=hein.journals/temple84&div=14&g_sent=1&casa_token=&collection=journals

Wallace, R. (2014). Modding: Amateur authorship and how the video game industry is actually getting it right. *Brigham Young University Law Review, 2014,* 219–256. https://digitalcommons.law.byu.edu/cgi/viewcontent.cgi?article=2915&context=lawreview

Walsh, K. (2014, October 11). *Nintendo updates take WII-U hostage until you agree with new legal terms.* Electronic Frontier Foundation. https://www.eff.org/deeplinks/2014/10/nintendo-updates-take-wii-u-hostage-until-you-agree-new-legal-terms

Ward v. Rock Against Racism, 491 U.S. 781 (1989).

Warren, S., & Brandeis, L. (1890). Right to privacy. *Harvard Law Review, 4,* 193–220. https://www.cs.cornell.edu/~shmat/courses/cs5436/warren-brandeis.pdf

Watters v TSR, Inc., 904 F.2d 378, 379 (6th Cir. 1990).

Weaver, J. F. (2015, February 25). *Who's responsible when a Twitter bot sends a threatening tweet?* Slate. http://www.slate.com/blogs/future_tense/2015/02/25/who_is_responsible_for_death_threats_from_a_twitter_bot.html.

Weins, K. (2015, April 21). We can't let John Deere destroy the very idea of ownership. *WIRED.* https://www.wired.com/2015/04/dmca-ownership-john-deere/

Weisbaum, G. (2017, November 28). *Hey Alexa, how secure are voice activated assistants like you?* NBC News. https://www.nbcnews.com/tech/security/hey-alexa-how-secure-are-voice-activated-assistants-you-n824566

Wendt v. Host International, Inc, 125 F.3d 806 (9th Cir. 1997).

Whipps, H. (2008, May 26). How Gutenberg changed the world. *Livescience.* https://www.livescience.com/2569-gutenberg-changed-world.html

White v. Samsung Electronics. Am. 971 F.2d 1395 (9th Cir. 1992).

Why video games are so expensive to develop. (2014, Sept. 25). *The Economist.* https://www.economist.com/the-economist-explains/2014/09/24/why-video-games-are-so-expensive-to-develop

Why Washington is turning on Silicon Valley. (2018, September 23). *The Week.* http://theweek.com/articles/726004/why-washington-turning-silicon-valley

Wickman, F. (2012, June 26). *May I suggest a revision?* Slate. http://www.slate.com/articles/news_and_politics/explainer/2012/06/aca_supreme_court_decision_how_do_the_justices_actually_write_their_opinions_.html

Wiedey, B. (2018, July 10). *NCAA Football: Why video game series hasn't returned five years after last release.* Sporting News. https://www.sportingnews.com/us/ncaa-football/news/ncaa-football-video-game-series-return-ncaa-19-obannon-ea-sports-possible-resolution/1qpe2ho9we8wli6w4qnm7t65ib

Willett, M. (2018, November 8). These 15 sci-fi books predicted the future. *Business Insider.* https://www.businessinsider.com/books-predicted-future-sci-fi-2018-11.

Wilson, M. (2017, July 14). AI inventing languages humans can't understand. Should we stop it? *Fast Company.* https://www.fastcompany.com/90132632/ai-is-inventing-its-own-perfect-languages-should-we-let-it

Wilson v. Midway Games, Inc., 198 F. Supp.2d 167 (D. Conn. 2002).

Wingfield, N. (2018, May 22). Amazon pushes facial recognition to police. Critics see surveillance risk. *New York Times.* https://www.nytimes.com/2018/05/22/technology/amazon-facial-recognition.html

Wood, L. L. & Hirokawa, C. F. (2000). Shot by the messenger: Rethinking media liability for violence induced by extremely violent publications and broadcasts. *Northern Kentucky Law Review, 27,* 47–66. https://chaselaw.nku.edu/content/dam/chase/docs/lawreview/v27/nklr_v27n1.pdf

Woodyatt, L. (2015, April 8). *The power of public shaming, for good and for ill.* The Conversation. https://theconversation.com/the-power-of-public-shaming-for-good-and-for-ill-38920

Wu, T. (2013, April 15). The oligopoly problem. *The New Yorker.* https://www.newyorker.com/tech/annals-of-technology/the-oligopoly-problem

Yakowicz, W. (2015, September 8) *Companies lose $400 billion to hackers each year.* INC. https://www.inc.com/will-yakowicz/cyberattacks-cost-companies-400-billion-each-year.html

Yakubowicz v. Paramount Pictures Corp., 536 N.E.2d 1067, 1070–72 (Mass. 1989).

Zacchini v. Scripps-Howard Broadcasting Co., 433 U.S. 562 (1977).

Zenor, J. (2015). Damming the leaks: Balancing national security, whistleblowing and the public interest. *Lincoln Memorial Law Review, 3,* 61–90. https://digitalcommons.lmunet.edu/cgi/viewcontent.cgi?article=1057&context=lmulrev

Zenor, J. (2016). A reckless disregard for the truth? The constitutional right to lie in politics. 38 *Campbell Law Review* 41.

Zimmerman, D. (2012). The "new" privacy and the "old": Is applying the tort law of privacy like putting high-button shoes on the internet? *Communication Law & Policy, 17*(2), 107–113.

Index

CPSIA information can be obtained
at www.ICGtesting.com
Printed in the USA
LVHW081640200122
709000LV00014B/1217